Little Flowers of Francis of Assisi

Little Flowers
of Francis of Assisi

A New Translation
by ROBERT H. HOPCKE
& PAUL A. SCHWARTZ

FOREWORD BY RICHARD ROHR, O.F.M.

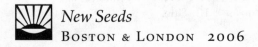

New Seeds
BOSTON & LONDON 2006

New Seeds Books
An imprint of Shambhala Publications, Inc.
Horticultural Hall
300 Massachusetts Avenue
Boston, Massachusetts 02115
www.newseedsbooks.com

9 8 7 6 5 4 3 2 1

First Edition
Printed in the United States of America

⊗This edition is printed on acid-free paper that meets
the American National Standards Institute z39.48 Standard.

Distributed in the United States by Random House, Inc.,
and in Canada by Random House of Canada Ltd

Designed by Graciela Galup

Library of Congress Cataloging-in-Publication Data
Fioretti di San Francesco. English.
Little flowers of Francis of Assisi: a new translation / by Robert H.
Hopcke and Paul A. Schwartz; foreword by Richard Rohr.—1st ed.
p. cm.
ISBN-13: 978-1-59030-375-7 (pbk.: alk. paper)
ISBN-10: 1-59030-375-X
1. Francis, of Assisi, Saint, 1182–1226. I. Hopcke, Robert H.,
1958– II. Schwartz, Paul, 1956– III. Title.
BX4700.F63E5   2006
271'.302—dc22

When I found your words, I devoured them; they became my joy and the happiness of my heart, because I bore your name, O Lord, God of hosts.

JEREMIAH 15:16

CONTENTS

FOREWORD

I HAVE BEEN A FRANCISCAN for forty-five years, trying to live up to the vision and practice of this larger-than-life (and larger-than-death!) man, called Francis of Assisi. I am told that he has the longest library bibliography of any person in history. He has a long list of would-be imitators too, most of us highly unsuccessful.

We usually read the *Little Flowers* once or twice while we are in initial formation, but not much afterward. We eventually look for the more objective, historical, and critical accounts of his life, hoping that we will find him a bit more imitable and practical. Not so. Never so.

Thus I am most grateful for this new abridged translation, because the *Little Flowers* is in a category all its own. It is like the collected sayings of the Buddha or the Zen masters, the stories of the Desert Fathers and Mothers, or the Midrashic collections of the rabbis. Don't get lost in the seemingly romantic details or language; don't let your historical-critical mind alone read the text; and don't start with "Is this realistic?"or even, "Do *I* like this?" (as if my first reactions should be normative). Those are all of the natural resistances of the small self and the controlling mind. The fundamentalist of any stripe always whittles the text down to his own limited knowability, and then either dismisses it—or pretends that she actually understands it. This is killing religion, worldwide. There will be no spiritual journey or spiritual growth in these cases.

And yes, the *Little Flowers* might seem too thirteenth century, too Catholic, too Italian! All of this is true. That is the container in which Saint Francis lived out his spiritual adventure. (There is no such thing as a value-free position!) But don't get trapped inside this container, because he was not trapped there himself, at least not totally. Any less than we are trapped in our own moment, our own culture, and our own context. Let's hope that later centuries will be as kind to us as I ask you to now be with him. Then he can thrill you! And then he can threaten you—in the way that saints, mystics, and prophets threaten us all.

I write this forward with very few words. After all, it is a spiritual master that you came to seek, not the warm-up act. And he himself taught not by words, but by actions, events, parables, and songs. These became his bouquet of flowers that he now hands on to another grateful age.

FRIAR RICHARD ROHR, O.F.M.
Center for Action and Contemplation
Albuquerque, New Mexico

INTRODUCTION

AT THE HEART of every Christian's faith is a longing, a natural human longing that is in a way inevitable. If one believes that God chose to be revealed in Jesus, a man who lived a life like ourselves—who had a rich circle of family, friends, and disciples about him as he ate, drank, slept, wept, and carried on his ministry, and who finally experienced the suffering of a state execution ending in physical death—how can any of us not feel a longing to have been there, to have actually, physically accompanied him in his earthly life? Among those of us who have known Jesus in spirit and in sacrament, who has not at some point in our reveries wondered how it would be to actually grasp his hand in the storm, like Peter; or to serve him a lunch made with love and devotion at our own kitchen table, like Martha; or perhaps to recline against his chest and smell the fragrance of him, washed clean, as did the Beloved Disciple at their final Passover meal together? If given the chance, would we not, like Mary, spend our savings to anoint him with spice, wrap him in crisp linen for his burial, and walk through the wet garden at dawn seeking him in grief and despair? Would we not, if he were before us now, take our own fingers and explore his wounded side, like Thomas; would we not cup our hands, blow on the coals of our bonfire, and cook him some fish as the calm waves of the lakeshore glisten in the morning sun?

The heart of the Christian faith is the incarnation, the experience of God made human in Jesus Christ. Our common humanity with God has planted within us as Christians an implacable but wholly understandable nostalgia to know Christ now, in our actual physical person, in our lives, through our senses. Because of this nostalgia, this memory infused with incarnational imagination, Christianity has always held itself to be a religion of saints, a community of people alive each day to being rendered into the living Body of Christ, through grace, through sacrament, through a perfecting of soul and spirit. In response to that deep longing born of God's incarnation, Christians are alert to ways in which Jesus is risen not back then, at some distant point in history, but rather right now, today, in our own personhood and in the people around us.

Of course, when we look to ourselves, too frequently, we see how far short from sanctity we have fallen, how we have missed the mark or fumbled the opportunities to reincarnate Christ in a more integrated way in our own humble lives. But sometimes, through our desire to see and touch the risen Christ once again, we are privileged to encounter certain individuals among us who are farther along in their paths toward wholeness, in whom we see much, much more clearly the image of God in Christ. In these people, we see and feel Jesus alive; in their authenticity, in their unique human natures as perfected by grace, God comes to earth, to us, once again. So our penchant for telling stories of those people in whom Christ was born, lived, and died again, this perennial hagiographic impulse of Christianity, so to speak, is inevitably part and parcel of our faith in a risen, incarnate God.

The *Little Flowers of Saint Francis*, a cycle of fifty-some stories about Francis of Assisi and his followers, is arguably one of the most classic expressions of this impulse that Christians possess. This collection of folk tales, legends, miracle stories, and narratives concerning Francis and his followers was given the title *Fioretti di San Francesco d'Assisi*, or *Little Flowers of Saint Francis*, and appeared in manuscripts somewhere in the early fourteenth century, that is, about seventy-five years after the death of Francis himself in 1226. For this reason, scholarly opinion seems to be that the *Fioretti* put to paper various stories in the oral tradition concerning Francis and the early Franciscans that had been circulating during his lifetime and afterward, much like the Gospels themselves. Scholars continue to debate whether the vernacular Tuscan Italian text preceded the formal Latin version—which appears to be a more probable scenario, given the popular nature and piety of the legends—or whether an original Latin text, now lost, was only afterward translated into vernacular Italian.

In either case, it is the Tuscan Italian text that is known and loved in Italy as a classic example of the beautiful vernacular prose of that era. Its purpose is dual, literary and religious, setting down a definitive version of oral stories that had been told for nearly a half-century concerning the holy man Francis and his followers, so as to make manifest the way in which Christ Jesus had risen and lived in the lives of Francis and his followers. Fortuitously for us, it is this Tuscan dialect that eventually became the basis for modern Italian, thus making the text of the *Little Flowers* an accessible and altogether enchanting example of early Italian literature. Indeed, anyone fluent in modern Italian can pick up this six-hundred-year-old text and read it with a certain ease, after becoming acquainted with a few idiosyncrasies of grammar, syntax, and vocabulary. Since the Italian vernacular text of the *Little Flowers* emerged from an oral tradition and was put down in writing precisely to be circulated among individuals without a high degree of literary education, the beautiful poetic style of the Italian vernacular text is especially clear, direct, and readable, narrative prose that is, in the words of one commentator, the very definition of "limpid." Along with those other classics of medieval Tuscan, Dante's *Divine Comedy*, Petrarca's *Sonnets,* and Boccaccio's *Decameron,* the *Little Flowers of Saint Francis* has long been a mainstay for any serious Italian language student.

However, the literary and linguistic importance of this text has, for generations of Italian students, frequently overshadowed its essentially religious intentions, which is quite unfortunate. In underemphasizing or completely ignoring the frankly spiritual aims of the redactor of these folktales, the most important aspect of this classic is lost, for these folktales were told of Francis *because* of Francis's holiness. Their religious and spiritual content *is* their very reason for being.

One, perhaps lamentable, feature of hagiography as a literary genre is at times a penchant for hyperbole, and in our cynical postmodern age, overblown descriptions and exaggerated flights of narrative fancy now do the opposite of what they might have done for earlier, simpler readers. Rather than inspire belief, hagiographic excesses now serve to impugn reliability and arouse suspicion. Nevertheless, from the standpoint of Christian history, and in particular, the history of the Roman Catholic Church itself, it is hard to overstate the singular effect that Francis of Assisi had on our Church and its spiritual culture, and even at a remove of over eight centuries, it is possible to read the general outlines of the life of Francis with some accuracy from the accounts given by his two earliest biographers, Thomas da Celano and Saint Bonaventure.

Giovanni Bernardone, renamed Francesco by his father, was born in 1181 to Pietro Bernardone, a rich cloth merchant in the small provincial town of Assisi (interestingly, the town is *Ascesi* in Tuscan Italian, literally "ascents," making it an apt place, literally and figuratively, for the manifestations of holiness.) Francis's early life was what might have been expected, then or now, of a spoiled young man with too much money and too much time on his hands in a small, boring, out-of-the-way provincial town, and naturally, his biographers make much of his dissolute, youthful character for their own pious purposes. All the same, it doesn't really strain credulity too much to imagine Francis going about doing what red-blooded, well-heeled, Italian twenty-something males are doing in small-town *piazze* all over Italy to this very day: showing off their to-the-minute-fashionable clothes, drinking and eating in loud, raucous parties with their friends to the wee hours of the morning at restaurants and cafés, and of course, chasing girls, girls, girls.

For Francis, as for many of us as we grow toward midlife, the transitory nature of all these youthful pleasures of the flesh began to become clear, first, after he suffered through a long illness in his twenty-fifth year, around 1204, an experience which in turn touched off a slow process of inward spiritual conversion for him and eventually culminated in a series of dramatic public gestures that would become the stuff of his legend. Given immortal form by Giotto's frescoes painted on the walls of the Upper Basilica of Assisi, these events—Francis's turning back on the road after setting out to war in Apulia; giving away his earthly possessions, cloak, horse, and money; and stripping himself naked before his uncomprehending father and his bishop in renunciation of wealth and social status—all signaled the beginning of his religious life as he turned to live as a poor man and devote himself to the service of the poor and the sick, notably lepers. After a vision in which the crucifix in the church of San Damiano spoke to him, saying, "Francis, go, repair my house which, as you see, is falling completely to ruin," he began to rebuild the literal church building with his own hands as a symbol, not especially hard to read, of a spiritual renewal of the larger Church that was to begin through his example of a radical return to evangelical Christianity.

These dramatic outward signs of Francis's initial conversion, however, soon resolved themselves into an ongoing way of life that was centered upon certain spiritual values and in which his holiness came to consist. He dedicated himself to living in poverty and in service as a mode of spiritual detachment, purification, and reliance upon God's providence. He affirmed God's love and delight in all aspects of his creation, which resulted in his founding religious communities for men, women, and laypeople as a mode of putting into affective practice the covenental love shown by the Lord to his people. With his companions, he lived a life of iterant mendicancy, traveling throughout the country preaching, teaching, exhorting, comforting, and healing, and it is these episodes of the middle years of Francis's active ministry, so to speak, that make up the bulk of the *Little Flowers* to follow.

Thus, one might say that these folktales are what, indeed, Christian hagiography always is: the comprehensive presentation of the life of a saint. In this case, it is the presentation of Francis of Assisi, living his life in God through Jesus Christ, and as such, quite self-consciously using the life of Jesus as presented in the Gospels as his model, as every Christian, in some ways, is called to do in his or her own life of devotion and ministry. His life, thus, represents an answer to the perennial question, "What is a saint?" In Francis's case, his sanctity is the result of life made intentionally transparent by means of contemplative prayer—a radical ascetic detachment from self, balanced by a warm and affectionate love for all of God's creation—and this transparency let all who knew him experience, through him, the living Christ as once again as alive in their own lives.

Likewise, as the *Little Flowers* amply and continuously illustrate, Francis's life in Jesus Christ, and particularly the last two years of it, represents an answer to the even more difficult question, "What is a mystic?" His gradual and increasing union with God, the transcendent source of all being, came to be reflected more and more by a multitude of mystical gifts narrated by these stories—inspired knowledge, ecstatic rapture, miraculous healings, and most especially his radical identity with Christ Crucified. Indeed, Francis's spiritual oneness with the Crucified Christ frames his whole biography, from the crucifix in San Damiano that called him to rebuild the church in ruins at the beginning of his religious life to the long account at the end of the *Little Flowers* wherein is described his reception of the stigmata, the five wounds of Jesus on the Cross, Francis's very body becoming for the first time in Christian tradition the literal, living image of the Crucified Savior.

In short, for all their narrative charm and literary grace, the stories of the *Little Flowers* are at their core a representation of nothing less than the Gospel through the lived example of Francis. They are a compendium of the core of Jesus's teaching, made vivid through persuasive and touching examples of Christian values lived in the real world with real people. They do what the Gospels were written to do: bring the risen Christ into the lives of all who hear these stories.

The title itself, so easily misread as a gratuitous literary decoration, is actually a powerful and multileveled theological statement, as one begins to understand after reading the stories. Certainly the most obvious level of how these stories are "little flowers" (*fioretti* in Italian, from the Latin *floretum*) is that each of them represents a specific example of the beauty of the life of Saint Francis and his followers, brought together in this collection as a kind of bouquet. Now, flowers were popular in the imagination of the Middle Ages: a similar floral image underlies the devotion of the rosary, a collection of prayers cast as individual "flowers" brought together in a kind of "garland" or "garden," which came into its current form more or less during the same period of time, and the use of floral imagery in places like Notre Dame or Chartres remain even today highpoints of European art.

However, why not simply call this collection the "jewel-box" or "tapestry" of Saint Francis? Wouldn't any other image denoting a collection of individual objects of beauty serve just as well? Simply, no, for this image drawn from nature is especially well-suited to entitle a collection of stories concerning a spiritual master who left the city, stripped him-self of the trappings of civilization, and went repeatedly to live as simply as possible in the midst of the natural world. To call these tales "little flowers" is especially appropriate for Francis, who embodied a creation theology all his own.

But here, we see yet another level of the title's meaning, for indeed, the content of these stories—the miracles, the teach-ings, the actions, the wisdom—are also "little flowers," that is to say, the individual efflorescences of his relationship with God. Put less technically, the stories present to us what blos-somed forth from his contemplative union with the Lord, and in calling them such, the symbol reminds us that, as delight-ful or inspiring as the flower itself might be, God is the ground in which his life—and ours—is rooted and draws its capacity to blossom. "Faith without works is dead," we hear in the letter of James, but Francis restates this same point in a more positive fashion in his example and in the image of the flower given to us by this collection: any authentic spiritual path always blooms into transformative action, sends out a fragrance that attracts and intoxicates those who come into contact with it, and, necessarily, inevitably, puts forth the true, nourishing fruit of good works, justice, and community.

And finally, of course, the title also refers to the simple, humble people with whom Francis spends his life and to whom he ministers. As the alert reader cannot fail to notice, the ecclesiastical grandees of the Roman Catholic Church are given very little space in this collection. Rather, it is always the "little flowers," normal people, everyday folks, the towns-people, peasants, workers, and women, who take center stage throughout, making these "folk tales" in every sense. Never himself ordained a priest, Francis, through his life and his foundation of a religious order intentionally described as "minor," represents one of the most persuasive, if not subversively radical, proponents of an ecclesiology fully inclusive of the laity that the Roman Catholic Church ever entertained before the reforms of the Second Vatican Council. Those who followed Francis's example are the true little flowers here, and it is through him that their life in God flourishes.

So, lest the reader think the title "Little Flowers" is merely an idle, decorative fillip placed on top of a sweet and charming collection of saintly legends, we feel confident that the stories themselves—little flowers in all the above ways—show how Francis's spirituality, theology, and ministry was very much a lived incarnation of the Gospel message and the seed out of which an inclusive, powerful renewal of the institutional Church was begun, literally, from the ground up. This particular translation of the *Little Flowers*, therefore, was undertaken with the firm intention of keeping all of the spiritual and theological aspects of Francis's life, as discussed above, in the forefront.

A number of complete translations of the *Little Flowers* exist in English already, and neither of us felt that there was any need to bring out another. The most recent, from the third volume of the three-volume set, *Francis of Assisi: Early Documents*, edited by Franciscan scholars Regis J. Armstrong, J. A. Wayne Hellmann, and William J. Short (New York: New City Press, 2001), provides an accurate and contemporary update to the version in the earlier omnibus *Saint Francis of Assisi: Writings and Early Biographies*, edited by Marion A. Habig (Chicago: Franciscan Herald Press, 1973). Along with these is the stand-alone monograph *Little Flowers of Saint Francis* from Raphael Brown (New York: Garden City, 1958). For our part, we used the Italian text as provided in *I fioretti di san Francesco*, edited by Guido Davico Bonino (Torino: Einaudi, 1998), as the basis for this translation.

Our intention here, therefore, is very specific: rather than provide what all the above have already provided—careful, scholarly, competent versions of the complete *Little Flowers* in English—we seek to highlight Francis of Assisi as a spiritual teacher in the model of Christ by way of storytelling in plain, everyday language, and we do this by way of a less scholarly and somewhat more creative approach to translating these tales. Our hope is to renew a direct acquaintance with Francis among those Christians who may not have spent much time with this particular spiritual master recently and also to bring the wisdom, power, and beauty of his life in God to those who are followers of other spiritual paths.

For this reason, we have chosen to present only those stories within the entire collection of the *Little Flowers* that clearly and forcefully present some sort of discrete spiritual teaching by Francis himself, roughly about half of the fifty-three stories in the original collection. Modern readers may be impressed by how many of these tales share an underlying spiritual kinship with other religious traditions; some have a paradoxical, Zen koan-like structure, while others center on universal spiritual themes, such as mastery of egotism and radical detachment from material possessions, termed "humility" and "poverty," respectively, within our Christian tradition.

In addition, we chose to include stories that revolve around some striking image or symbol, in the form of a miracle, dream, vision, or healing, either in Francis's own life or in the lives of his closest companions. These stories are near-perfect examples of the European folktale and, as such, they are saturated with unusual archetypal symbolism that we believe give a readership beyond a Christian audience a great deal to savor and contemplate. By bringing all this unconventional and even challenging imagery to modern readers—Francis stripping himself naked and standing in the midst of the flames before a female seductress, telling Leo to shit in the mouth of the Devil, the Pope himself enjoining Clare to bless the bread, which then manifests the sign of the Cross—we hope to counteract a view of Franciscan spirituality that has become sentimental or narrowly pietistic and recover the radical transformative edge of what Francis, and Jesus, preached and taught.

As for what we omitted from the original collection, those stories were of principally two types—accounts of various institutional events pertaining to the early days of the Order or stories about various Franciscan saints following Francis's death. While these stories are certainly important from a scholarly point of view, we felt that this material was of limited interest to a more general audience and not always as spiritually edifying, nor of the same literary caliber, as the stories we have chosen to include. Any readers interested in this material we encourage to seek out the above-referenced translations.

In keeping with our overall intentions, therefore, we have quite deliberately cast the text into contemporary American English and eschewed the mannered "wherefore art thou" language of translations that attempt, we feel misguidedly, to lend a kind of pseudoantique tone to the English version. The original Italian was in the vernacular—very clear, very graphic, and indeed, at times quite vulgar. Similarly, in spotlighting Francis's spiritual teaching, we have consistently and very consciously chosen throughout the text not to render literal, one-for-one translations of certain terms or words but instead have worked to creatively recast certain words or expressions in ways that make clear the underlying spiritual or theological meaning for a contemporary American. *Penitenza* is, for example, rendered not simply as "penitence," but as "conversion of life," which is, after all, the endpoint of any penitential practice. *Divozione* in all its forms we did not render as mere "devotion" but variously as "faith," "love," or "dedication," depending on the context, since superficial pieties seemed to us less important than the underlying attitude. For a mature and sophisticated American readership with a capacity for understanding the nature of evil beyond simplistic personifications, we decided that "the Evil One" or "the Enemy" was the more expressive, conceptually accurate translation for *demonio* than "the Devil" would be.

As the Italian expression has it, *tradurre tradire*—"a translation is always a betrayal"—and so translators are always faced with hard, imperfect choices between the literal text, the cultural context, the connotative meaning, and the needs of an intended audience. Because with a text like the *Little Flowers* a sufficient number of literally accurate translations exist, we decided throughout this version to plump for the cultural, conceptual, and connotative aspects of the text with an eye toward a special readership interested primarily in Francis's spiritual wisdom.

We have also added introductory comments to each of the stories included to draw the reader's attention to certain notable aspects of the story and to foster an attitude of reflectiveness. In keeping with the spiritual intention behind this abridged edition of the *Little Flowers,* we are hoping that the reader will not simply breeze through these tales as if they were mere literal biographic sketches, for clearly they are not and cannot be. Rather, they are little gems of Christian "wisdom literature," developed to be told and retold as a tool for gaining insight, enriching contemplation, and practicing prayerful, imaginative presence with God.

The result of these choices, we hope, is a unique contribution to Franciscan literature and a faithful recreation of what the *Little Flowers* have been throughout the centuries: one way that the life of Jesus Christ, as reflected in Francis, can enliven our own lives and call us each to a greater detachment from self and to a fuller and more constant delight in creation and providence. We doubt that anyone, regardless of spiritual tradition, can read these stories and *not* be inspired to ever deeper love of God and neighbor. And in this way, these *Little Flowers,* though very Italian, very Christian, very medieval, are Francis's gift across the centuries to the soul of the modern world.

Little Flowers of Francis of Assisi

one

In the name of our crucified Lord Jesus Christ and his virgin mother Mary. This book is a collection of little flowers, that is, miracles and examples of devotion given to us by Saint Francis, glorious in his poverty, and by certain of his holy companions. May Jesus Christ be praised. Amen. ⊰⊱

From this first chapter, the reader is shown that Jesus's life and ministry are the model for Francis's life and ministry. Given this explicit statement, the question might arise: is this imitation of Christ a literary conceit on the part of the author, or does it genuinely reflect Francis's own spirituality? In that all of Francis's religious life can be seen as a slow, mystical absorption into the person and experience of the Lord, this first chapter is clearly more an enunciation of what one might call Francis's theology—how he understood and lived his life in Christ—than a mere literary introduction.

✦ ✦ ✦

WE MUST FIRST UNDERSTAND that our glorious father, Saint Francis, conformed his life in all ways to our blessed Lord Jesus Christ. Like Christ, who at the beginning of his active ministry chose twelve apostles and enjoined them to turn away from all worldly things so as to imitate him in his

1

poverty and all other spiritual virtues, so, too, Saint Francis chose to found the Order with twelve companions deeply devoted to poverty. And, just as one of the twelve apostles, Judas Iscariot by name, renounced his vocation and betrayed Christ, and hanged himself by the neck, so, too, one of the twelve companions of Saint Francis, Giovanni della Cappella by name, renounced his vocation and hanged himself as well, becoming an example to all the rest who, in humility and holy fear, understood that, in the life of faith, no one is certain to persevere to the end. And as the first apostles became known throughout the world for the wonder of their holiness and humility, full of the Holy Spirit, likewise, the holy companions of Saint Francis were men of a sanctity that had not been seen in the world since the days of those first apostles.

Indeed, the Lord saw fit to take Brother Giles up to heaven in rapture, as he had Saint Paul; and yet another, Brother Philip the Tall, like the prophet Isaiah, had his lips anointed with a burning coal by the Lamb of God. Brother Silvester conversed with God in all familiarity, as one would with a friend, as Moses had in earlier days; and soaring like the majestic eagle, the symbol of John the Evangelist, Brother Bernardo entered into the light of Divine Wisdom through the subtlety of his insight and was able, thereby, to lay bare the true inner meaning of Holy Scripture to all who heard him. Sanctified by God in heaven while living yet on earth was Brother Ruffino, nobleman of Assisi. Thus, each of them were granted signs of holiness and favor, as the following account will show.

two

Of Brother Bernardo of Quintavalle, Saint Francis's first companion. ⊷

This story of Bernardo's conversion and ministry exemplifies that mainstay of Catholic homily quotes attributed to Francis, "Preach the Gospel, and when necessary, use words." For the record, this quote is not found in any of his writings, though in his Rule he did exhort the brothers to preach "by their deeds." In any case, this principle is certainly his; to proclaim the Good News by one's own actions is the powerful core of Franciscan spirituality. The qualities of patience, humility, submission, and material detachment are exemplified not just in the content of the story but in the very fact that the first lengthy account here is not about Francis at all but about his companions. Just as he sneaks away in the night for intimacy with God, likewise here his figure recedes into the background to allow Bernardo center stage, yet again an example of humility.

⁂

THE FIRST COMPANION chosen by Saint Francis was Brother Bernardo of Assisi, whose conversion occurred in the following way. Though still living as a layman at the time, Francis had nevertheless turned away from the ways of this world and had given himself over so fully to a life of mortification and penance that his family and friends, as well as strangers who encountered him, took him for a madman. Despised and rejected, he had stones and mud thrown at him wherever he went, and yet he bore this contempt and these insults as if he were deaf, dumb, and blind, saying nothing and enduring it all with patience. It was this patience of his in the face of such utter contempt, his complete and total renunciation of the world, that drew the attention of Bernardo, a member of one of the most noble and learned families in Assisi. Over the course of two years, he witnessed how Francis bore the unremitting spite and physical insults of their fellow townsfolk with an unwavering faith and without complaint, until Bernardo eventually said to himself, "Only a man graced by God could behave in such a fashion." So, he invited Francis to be his houseguest and to share his table, in order to more fully understand such holiness as he had seen in him.

That first night, Bernardo made a bed for Francis in his own room, where he kept a lamp burning throughout the night, but Francis, in order to conceal his sanctity, quickly threw himself on the bed and made it appear that he was sleeping, waiting until Bernardo, who had also lain down, finally began to snore loudly. Only then did Francis, thinking Bernardo fast asleep, arise and begin to pray, raising his eyes and his hands toward heaven with deep devotion and fervor, repeating, "My God, my God . . ." over and over again, weeping in the darkness until the first light of day. This prayer was his only prayer that night, "My God, my God . . . ," and in it he became caught up in wonder and in the contemplation of the divine majesty of God who so loved the world that he came into this realm of death, to save not only his poor, humble servant Francis but, by the light of the Holy Spirit, many others of this world as well through him. Endowed with a spirit of prophecy, Francis was given to see all the great things that God would do by way of him and his Order, and so, painfully aware of his own inadequacies and faltering virtues, he called upon God over and over in his prayer that night, asking for his mercy and his power to sustain his human weakness and to help him accomplish the great work he was to do. But Bernardo was not asleep, and by the light of the lamp, he could see Francis's prayers and his devotion, and, feeling himself profoundly moved by what he saw, the Holy Spirit touched his soul that night, and he was inspired to a conversion of life.

When morning came, Bernardo called to Saint Francis and said, "Brother Francis, I say to you, from the depths of my heart, I am completely ready to follow you, to renounce the world and to do anything you ask of me." Hearing this, Saint Francis felt his spirit leap in joy, and he replied, "Bernardo, your commitment here is an act both great and difficult. So together we must first take counsel from our Lord Jesus Christ and ask him to show his will and pleasure and to instruct us how to carry out your intention. Let us go, then, to the bishop's residence where we will find a good priest to say Mass for us, after which we will spend the morning in prayer, until the third hour, when we will open the missal three times and in this fashion, the Lord can show us how he has chosen for us to proceed."

After Mass, then, and having spent the morning in prayer, the priest, at the request of Saint Francis, made the sign of the Cross over the missal and opened the book three times in the name of Jesus Christ. The first time they were shown the words of our Lord Jesus Christ to the rich young man in the Gospel: "If you wish to be perfect, go, sell all that you have, give it to the poor, and come, follow me." The second time they were shown the words of Christ who, as he sent his apostles out to preach, said to them, "Take nothing with you on the road, neither walking stick nor purse, neither shoes nor money," so that they might learn to put all their faith and hope in the providence of God and have no other intention but to preach the Good News to all people. The third time the missal was opened, they read the words of Christ, who said, "If you wish to come with me, deny yourself, take up your cross, and follow me."

Saint Francis then said to Bernardo, "This is the counsel that Christ gives us today. Go then and do all that you have been told to do. Blessed be our Lord Jesus Christ who has deigned to show us how to live the Gospel." Hearing this, Bernardo indeed went and did as he was told. A very rich man, he sold everything he had, and with great joy gave it all away to the poor, widowed, and orphaned, to those in prison, to those living in monastic poverty, and to those ailing in the hospital and he was helped faithfully and generously in these actions by Saint Francis himself.

Now, a man named Silvestro, seeing just how much money Francis was giving away to the poor, was spurred on by greed. He went to Francis and said, "You know, you never fully paid me for the stones you used to repair the church. So now, since it looks like you have come into money, pay me what you owe." Amazed at such selfishness but seeking to follow the precepts of the Gospel in all things, Francis did not argue with the man. Rather, he put his hands into the bag of money Bernardo was carrying, drew out a handful, and gave it all to

Silvestro, telling him that if this were not enough, he would give him more still, should he ask.

Satisfied with this, Silvestro left and went home, but that evening, upon thinking about how he had behaved that day and considering Bernardo's fervor and Francis's holiness, he began to repent of his greed. That night and the following two nights, there came to him a vision of Saint Francis. In it, he saw a cross made of gold issuing from Francis's mouth, the top of which reached to heaven and the arms of which covered the whole of the world from east to west. Because of this vision, Silvestro woke up the next day and gave all he owned to the poor, joining the Friars Minor and growing in holiness and grace, speaking with God as easily and naturally as he would with a friend, conversations that Saint Francis himself often witnessed and that will be more fully recounted below.

Bernardo, too, was granted much grace by God and was often taken up in ecstatic contemplation, so Saint Francis spoke of him as worthy of all reverence and called him the founder of the Order, in that he was the first to have renounced the world and had held nothing back from the Lord's poor, embracing the poverty of the Gospel and offering himself, naked, to the arms of the Crucified Christ,

May he be blessed, now and forever. Amen.

three

How Saint Francis, having had evil thoughts against Brother Bernardo, ordered Bernardo to place his foot against his throat and mouth three times. ◄◄

The raw physicality of this story makes it especially striking among this collection, and we are presented here with certain symbolic images and themes that will continue throughout these tales. Francis's difficulties with his eyes and his eyesight, here attributed to his excessive penitential weeping, may well be a vestige of a real physical disability from which he actually suffered, since this affliction appears a number of times. Likewise, his gift for inspired knowledge and revelation is presented here as a very intimate, direct conversation with God. However, of most note, rather than playing role of the high and mighty Founder of an Order with his disciples, Francis continually uses his companions, as he does Bernardo here, to inflict mortification and correction upon himself. Francis the antihero is Francis the saint, a point we would all do well to remember about him and, the story suggests, in our own spiritual lives.

✳ ✳ ✳

SAINT FRANCIS, most devoted servant of the Crucified Christ, had been living a life of such severe penitence that his continuous weeping over his own sinfulness had left him

8

nearly blind. One day, having left his own house with a companion to go see Brother Bernardo and speak with him about holy matters, he found Bernardo in the woods, praying fervently, absorbed in union with God. Calling to him, Saint Francis said, "Come and speak to this blind man." But Brother Bernardo did not answer him, for his mind was drawn up to God so fully that nothing could disturb his contemplation. Though this indeed was Bernardo's most singular grace, as Francis himself now witnessed, nevertheless, he still wished to speak with Bernardo. Thus, a second and a third time he called to him, and yet Brother Bernardo heard nothing, neither answering nor going to Francis in response. Wondering to himself why Bernardo would ignore him in this way, Francis went away, somewhat sad, and, after having gone some distance while pondering this thought, he stopped and said to his companion, "Wait for me here."

Francis went off alone to a place of solitude, and, falling to his knees in prayer, he asked God to disclose to him why Bernardo had not answered him. There came to him a voice from God who said, "Oh poor little man, why are you so troubled? Should a man leave his God the Creator to attend instead to other men, mere creatures? Brother Bernardo was with me when you called him, and so he was not able to answer you or come to you nor even hear your words." At this response from God, Francis rose right away, and in great haste returned to the place where Bernardo had been praying so as to confess the wrong he had held against him in his mind.

Seeing Francis approach, Bernardo went to him and knelt before him. But this time, Francis had him rise to his feet and instead, feeling deep compunction, he told Bernardo of the resentful thoughts he had been entertaining against him and of what God had said to him in prayer. He ended by saying to Bernardo, "I command you, under holy obedience, to do as I say." Fearing that he would ask him to inflict upon Francis some excessive form of penance, as was often the case, Bernardo wished to avoid obeying him and so, said, "I am prepared to obey you, as long as you also promise to do whatever I tell you to do." Saint Francis agreed and promised to obey Bernardo in turn, so Bernardo then said, "Tell me, then, Father, what do you wish me to do?" to which Saint Francis replied, "I command you, under holy obedience, to punish my presumption and willfulness by placing one of your feet on my throat and the other on my mouth as I lie on the ground beneath you, and do this three times as you reproach and shame me by saying, 'Abase yourself, wicked son of Pietro Bernardoni, you miserable, prideful creature, why do you think so highly of yourself?'" Though it was difficult to do as he was asked, Brother Bernardo nevertheless, out of holy obedience, did as Francis had commanded him, standing upon his mouth and throat as gently as he could, after which, Saint Francis then said, "And now, command me as you will, to do as you say, for I have promised you obedience as well."

For his turn, Brother Bernardo said, "I command you, under holy obedience, each time that we are together, to reproach me severely for my faults and to impose correction on me for all my defects." Amazed at Brother Bernardo's sanctity, Francis held him in great esteem and found nothing in him to either correct or reproach, such that from that time forward, Saint Francis tried to avoid spending time with Bernardo, lest that under his promised obedience he would have to reproach Bernardo, whom he considered a holy man. When occasion would arise for Francis to see him or speak with him, Francis would afterward quickly leave, which inspired deep devotion in all who saw the affection, reverence, and humility with which our holy father Francis regarded his firstborn spiritual son Brother Bernardo.

All praise and glory to Christ Jesus and to his poor servant Francis. Amen.

four

How an angel of the Lord put a question to Brother
Elias, guardian of a community house in the valley of
Spoleto, who responded with arrogance and pride;
and how Brother Bernardo encountered the same
angel as he returned from San Giacomo. ⤙

Angels figure prominently throughout the Little Flowers, *and
usually they have the character we see in this tale—imperious,
challenging, beautiful—which is a more faithful representation of
how these messengers of the Most High appear in Scripture,
particularly Jewish Scripture, than current popular culture tends to
present them. The inquiry provoked by the angel and the depiction of
both Bernardo and Francis at a physical remove from the community
house suggest a spiritual subtext to the story. It can be read as a
cautionary tale concerning the dangers of living in an insulated
community where it can be easy to let ego and all its attendant
problems—anger, pride, pettiness, confusion, human customs—gain
the upper hand and thereby not to even recognize God when one
of his messengers is knocking loudly at one's door.*

⚜ ⚜ ⚜

IN THE EARLY DAYS of the Order, when there were still only
a few friars and many communities had not yet been estab-

lished, Saint Francis, out of devotion, went to San Giacomo di Galizia, taking with him several friars, among them Brother Bernardo. On the road together, he and the brothers came upon a poor, sick man, and moved with compassion, he said to Brother Bernardo, "My son, I would like you to stay here and tend to the needs of this ailing man." Brother Bernardo, humbly kneeling and bowing his head, received Francis's instruction obediently and stayed there with the sick man, while Saint Francis and the rest of the companions proceeded to San Giacomo. Upon their arrival, they spent the first night in prayer at the church there, where it was revealed to Saint Francis that he was to establish various communities throughout the world such that there would be a great multitude of friars serving the Lord and that the Order would greatly increase. In the light of this revelation, Saint Francis established a number of communities in that region, and on his way back, he found Brother Bernardo where he had asked him to stay. The sick man, whom he asked Bernardo to tend, was now completely healed.

Saint Francis allowed Brother Bernardo to accompany him to San Giacomo the following year, after which he returned to the valley of Spoleto without Bernardo and stayed for a time in an isolated place, along with Brother Masseo, Brother Elias, and several other friars. All of the friars took great care not to disturb Saint Francis while he was praying, out of the great reverence they bore toward him and because they knew that God frequently revealed wondrous things to him in prayer. One day, as Francis was praying in the woods, a handsome young man dressed for traveling came to the door of the community house, knocking so loudly and insistently for such a long time that the friars within wondered what would prompt anyone on earth to go about knocking in such a strange way. Brother Masseo went to the door and said to the young man, "My son, from the way you are banging on our door, you can't be from around here. Where are you from?"

The young man replied, "How is it, then, that I should be knocking? Tell me."

Brother Masseo said, "Knock three times in a row, then wait a bit, just enough time for a brother to recite an Our Father and come to greet you at the door. If, in this amount of time, he does not come, then knock once more."

The young man then answered. "Well, I'm in a great hurry, so that's why I was knocking the way I was. I have a long journey ahead, of me and I came here to speak with Saint Francis. But he is praying in the woods, and so I don't want to bother him. So I would like you to go and get Brother Elias for me so that I can ask him a question, because I've heard that he, too, is a very wise man."

So Brother Masseo went to fetch Brother Elias for the young man. However, Elias balked at being summoned in such a manner to a complete stranger and had no desire to go and talk with him. Not knowing what he should do or say to the young man, Brother Masseo decided to tell a fib and simply say, "Brother Elias cannot come to the door," thinking that if he were to say that "Brother Elias has no desire to see or talk to you," it would not look very good for him. In the meantime, as Brother Masseo thought about how to handle this situation, the young man began banging on the door loudly and insistently, as he had the first time, and when Masseo got back to the front door, he said to the young man, "You aren't following my clear instructions about door-knocking, my son." To which the young man answered, "Brother Elias does not want to see me. So I want you to go tell Brother Francis that, though I came to speak with him, I do not wish to disturb his prayer, and therefore, he should tell Elias to come and speak with me in his stead."

Brother Masseo went to Saint Francis, who was praying in the woods, eyes lifted to the heavens, and recounted to him the story of this young man's visit and Brother Elias's response. Perceiving that the young man was an angel of the Lord come to them in human form, Saint Francis did not move from where he was kneeling, nor did he take his eyes from the heavens, but instead he simply said to Brother Masseo, "Go and tell Brother Elias that he is to go and speak with this young man, under obedience."

Commanded, thus, under obedience by Saint Francis but nevertheless quite perturbed, Brother Elias went to the door of the community house and with obvious annoyance asked the young man, "So what do you want?"

The young man replied, "I hope, brother, that you haven't allowed yourself to be as annoyed as you appear, for after all, anger is a great hindrance to spiritual progress and clouds our ability to perceive what is true and good."

Brother Elias merely asked one more time, "Tell me what you want from me."

The young man asked, "I would like to know what you think. Are those who follow the Gospel of Jesus Christ permitted to eat whatever is placed before them, as Jesus himself instructed his disciples, and do you believe it is lawful to preach anything other than this freedom in the Gospel?"

Disdainfully, Brother Elias replied, "That's an easy question to answer, but I'm not in the mood to speak with you. Go about your business and stop bothering us."

The young man said, "I myself could probably answer the question better than you, then, eh?"

Hearing this, Brother Elias flew into an out-and-out rage, slammed the door in the young man's face, and walked away. However, later on, as he began to consider the question the young man had asked, he began to wonder if he was indeed right about the matter, as he had thought, and turned the question over in his mind. At the time he was serving as Vicar of the Order, and he began to question whether or not, by forbidding the brothers to eat meat, he had imposed a practice that in fact transgressed the Gospel or the Rule of Saint Francis. In fact, the more Brother Elias thought about it, the more it seemed that the young man had directed the question specifically at him. No longer sure that what he had done was right or good, he returned to the door, hoping to speak with the young man further and to clarify the matter, only to find that the young man had gone away. Elias realized then that, in his pride, he had made himself unworthy to speak with angels.

Upon his return from the woods, Saint Francis, to whom all things in heaven were revealed, strongly reproached Brother Elias for his actions, saying, "You have behaved very badly, Brother Elias, for in your arrogance you have driven away from our house the very angel that God has sent to teach us his ways. I will tell you now, I'm very afraid that this pride of yours will mean that you will not end your days in the Order." And indeed, as Saint Francis predicted, Brother Elias later left the Order and did not die a friar.

That same day, at the moment that the angel left, he appeared in the same form to Brother Bernardo, who was returning from San Giacomo and was on the banks of a large river. Greeting Bernardo in his own language, the angel said, "God's peace be upon you, good brother."

Astounded by the beautiful appearance of this young man and the peaceful, joyous manner of his greeting to him, the good brother Bernardo asked him, "Where are you from, young man?"

The angel answered, "I have just come from the place where Saint Francis lives. I had gone there to speak with him, but he was in prayer, rapt in contemplation of things divine, and I did not wish to bother him. There, too, live Brother Masseo, Brother Giles, and Brother Elias, and Brother Masseo was kind enough to instruct me on how to knock on the door the way it is done among the brothers. But Brother Elias did not want to speak with me about the question I wished to discuss, and even though later he repented of his refusal to see me or speak with me, by then it was too late."

After recounting these events, the angel then asked Brother Bernardo, "Why are you not crossing this river?"

Brother Bernardo answered him, saying, "Because I am afraid the water is much deeper than it appears."

The angel said, "Let us go together then. Have no fear," and after taking Bernardo's hand, in the blink of an eye, he placed him on the opposite bank of the river.

In this way, Bernardo knew that the young man was an angel of the Lord, and with great reverence and joy, he said in a loud voice, "O blessed angel of the Lord, tell me your name."

The angel replied, "Why do you ask my name, which is wonderful?" and at that, the angel disappeared, leaving Bernardo greatly consoled and rejoicing all the way home. He made special note of the day and the time that the angel had appeared to him, and when he came to the community house where Saint Francis and the other brothers were staying, he told them all that had happened. From this they realized that the angel that had visited them was the same angel that had visited Bernardo, and they gave thanks to God.

All praise to Jesus Christ and to Francis, poor man of God. Amen.

five

How Brother Bernardo of Assisi was sent by Saint Francis to Bologna to found a community there. ◂◂

As Bernardo himself was converted by Francis's example of patience in the face of public ridicule, so, too, Bernardo's example of the same brings forth much fruit in Bologna. For modern readers, these and other like descriptions of Francis and his followers may call to mind the all-too-familiar hooded, impoverished figures of the street people and panhandlers we ourselves pass by every day. Jesus and his followers, like Francis and his followers, were more like these poor on our streets than the rich, comfortable, and admired citizens of Bologna. Presenting Bernardo as a "stranger and pilgrim," a voluntary outcast of his own society, the story is not intended merely to recount the facts of a Franciscan mission to Bologna but also to take square aim at our own comfort and ease as inimical to our own wholeness. Sanctity is not a state of blissful spiritual perfection but the fruit of radical detachment and trenchant social critique lived on the streets.

✳ ✳ ✳

SAINT FRANCIS and his companions, having been called by God to carry the Cross of Christ in their hearts, to show it forth in their actions and to preach it with their tongues, thus showed themselves in their austere dress, actions, and speech—indeed, in all aspects of their lives—as men living an ongoing crucifixion to the world. For this reason, they more deeply desired to bear shame and insult for the love of Christ than any honor, reverence, or vain praise the world might offer, such that they rejoiced when they were reviled for their manner of life and were troubled when praised for their piety. They traveled the world as strangers and pilgrims, carrying nothing other than Christ Crucified with them, and because they were each branches of the true vine, that is, Christ, they produced good and abundant fruit in many souls whom they won over to God.

In the beginning of the Order, it happened that Saint Francis sent Brother Bernardo to Bologna so that there, according to the grace God had granted him, he might produce fruit pleasing to the Lord, and having made the sign of the Cross in holy obedience, Brother Bernardo left and journeyed to Bologna. However, when the children of the town saw Bernardo, his clothes poor and disheveled as those of a street person, they mocked and insulted him as if he were mentally deranged, but Brother Bernardo patiently and cheerfully bore all these insults for the love of Christ. Indeed, so that he might be tormented even further, he intentionally went to the main square of the town and sat down in plain view, whereupon a great crowd of townspeople and children gathered about him and began to mock him by pulling him around by his hood, this way and that, all the while throwing stones and dirt at him.

Brother Bernardo responded peacefully, patiently, and meekly, his face ever cheerful; many times he subjected himself to such public ridicule in the square. Because patience is a work of perfection and proof of virtue, Brother Bernardo's faithful, patient demeanor, by which it seemed he hardly noticed the daily abuse and insults, came to the attention of one of the lawyers in the town, who said to himself, "This man surely is a saint." Going to Bernardo one day, he asked him, "Who are you and why have you come here?"

Brother Bernardo answered him by reaching into his habit, pulling the Rule of Saint Francis out, and telling him to read it. As the man read, he was astounded at the high degree of spiritual wisdom contained therein, the way of perfection that it represented, such that he went about exclaiming to his friends, "Never before have I seen such devotion in the practice of religion. This man and his companions are without a doubt among the holiest of men in this world, and it is a great wrong to insult him in such a way, he whom we should honor as a true friend of God."

He then said to Brother Bernardo, "If you wish to establish a house here where you might fittingly serve God, I would willingly provide you with the means to do so, so that my own soul might grow in grace."

Brother Bernardo replied, "My dear sir, I believe that our Lord Jesus Christ himself has inspired you and so, I accept your offer with my whole heart in his honor."

This lawyer thus took Brother Bernardo into his own house and, with great joy and generosity, gave him the residence that he had promised, furnishing it at his own expense, becoming in this way a godfather and advocate to Brother Bernardo and his companions in Bologna.

Brother Bernardo soon became known and well esteemed by the people of the town for his inspired teaching, such that those who had occasion to see or touch him accounted themselves blessed. But being a true disciple of Christ and of humble Saint Francis, he began to fear that such worldly acclaim might impair his peace of mind and the health of his soul, and so, one day went to visit Saint Francis, saying, "Father, a house has been established in Bologna. Please send some friars there to stay and sustain it, for I have done what I can there and I fear that the high regard in which I am held there might well be the undoing all of that has been accomplished."

In hearing all the good things that had been done and the way in which God had acted through Brother Bernardo, Saint Francis gave thanks to the Lord and then began to scatter his poor disciples of the Cross more widely. He sent his brothers to Bologna and to Lombardy, and many communities were established in many places.

All praise and honor to Jesus Christ and to his poor servant Francis. Amen.

six

How Saint Francis, while dying, blessed holy Brother Bernardo and named him Vicar of the Order. ⤙

This short initial cycle of stories concerning Bernardo ends here with a recreation of the scene in Genesis, chapter 48, in which Jacob/Israel crosses his arms to bless the younger son, Ephraim over the older son, Manasseh. This story in Jewish Scripture harks back to the earlier story in Genesis, chapter 27, of Jacob's cleverness in obtaining his father Isaac's blessing over his brother, Esau. While Francis's poor eyesight is yet again used as part of the plot, the purpose of this story is similar to its Biblical antecedents: it puts forward humility toward others and submission to God's will as primary spiritual values within the Judeo-Christian tradition. "My ways are not your ways," says the Lord.

⁎ ⁎ ⁎

BROTHER BERNARDO was of such holiness that Saint Francis himself revered him and often praised him. One day, while absorbed in prayer, God revealed his will to Saint Francis, that Brother Bernardo would be engaged in quite a number of very fierce battles against various demons. Saint Francis, out of great compassion for Brother Bernardo, whom he loved like his own son, often wept and prayed to God that

Jesus Christ might help Bernardo to be victorious in his spiritual struggles against evil.

Once, in the midst of such devoted prayer, God spoke to Saint Francis, saying, "Francis, have no fear, for all the temptations assailing Bernardo have been permitted by God to help Bernardo toward a crown of great virtue and merit, for he indeed shares in the ministry of the kingdom of the heaven." Upon hearing this, Saint Francis rejoiced greatly and gave thanks to God, and from then on, held Bernardo in even greater reverence and love.

The esteem Saint Francis felt for Bernardo throughout his life he likewise demonstrated as he approached his death. It so happened that, toward the end of his life on this earth, Saint Francis, like the holy patriarch Jacob, was surrounded by his devoted sons, who were weeping over their impending loss of such a loving father. Seeing them about him, Saint Francis asked, "Where is my firstborn? Come to me, my son, so that my soul can bless you before I die." To which Brother Bernardo, out of earshot, said to Brother Elias, then Vicar of the Order, "Father, go and let the right hand of the saint bless you." Thus, Brother Elias drew near to the right hand of the saint, and Saint Francis, unable to see through his tears, placed his right hand upon Brother Elias's head.

"This is not my firstborn son, Brother Bernardo," he said, so Brother Bernardo drew near to the left hand of the saint. Saint Francis then crossed his arms, so that he might lay his right hand upon the head of Brother Bernardo and his left upon the head of Brother Elias, saying, "Brother Bernardo, having been chosen as firstborn in our holy Order to give an example of the Gospel way of life and to imitate Christ in his poverty, may the Father of our Lord Jesus Christ bless you with every spiritual blessing under the heavens. Not only have you given up all your possessions and distributed these freely and completely to all those in need, out of love for Christ, but you have further offered yourself up to God in this Order out of love. Thus, you have been blessed by our Lord Jesus Christ and by me, his poor servant, with eternal blessings in all that you do, in your travels, in your rest, whether awake or asleep, living or dying. All who bless you will themselves be blessed. All who curse you will not escape punishment. You shall be the head of all your brothers, and they shall obey your instructions. You may receive into this Order whomever you deem worthy. No brother shall have rule over you, and you may go wherever you wish."

After Saint Francis's death, the brothers venerated and loved Brother Bernardo as a revered father, and while on his own deathbed, brothers from all over the world came to him, including the divine and priestly Saint Giles, who, upon seeing Brother Bernardo, said with great joy, *"Sursum corda,* Brother Bernardo. Lift up your heart." And holy Brother Bernardo told one of the friars privately to provide Brother Giles with a place suitable for contemplative prayer, and it was so provided.

In his final hour, Brother Bernardo sat up and spoke to the brothers around him, saying, "Dearest brothers, I do not wish to say a great deal to you. The faith I lived in this Order, you, too, will live, and as I am dying now, so, too, shall you one day. Were I to have been offered a thousand lives equal to or better than the one that I have lived, I say to you today, from the depths of my soul, I would not have chosen other than I did—to live my life in service to our Lord Jesus Christ. Every offense I have committed, I now confess, and I throw myself before you upon the mercy of Jesus Christ my savior. I beg you, dearest brothers, love one another."

After these words and other wise teachings, Brother Bernardo lay back down upon his bed, whereupon his face shown with such exceedingly great happiness that the friars were amazed. In this state of blessed happiness, his holy soul, crowned with glory, passed from this life to the life of the angels in heaven.

Praise be to Jesus Christ and his poor servant Francis. Amen.

seven

Saint Francis observes Lent on an island in the Lake of Perugia, fasting forty days and forty nights, eating nothing but a bit of bread. ⤙

As the focus of the collection now moves more directly to the person of Francis, we see certain features of his spiritual life explicitly modeled on Jesus. These features are also presented to the reader as models for our own spiritual practice: silent, contemplative prayer in communion with nature; the voluntary assumption of physical mortification; and, in that seemingly small but singular detail of Francis's "imperfect" abstinence, a persuasive suggestion that we moderate our attempts toward spiritual perfection lest they foster that even more serious pitfall in the life of the soul: spiritual pride.

⁜⁜⁜

Saint Francis, true servant of Christ, was in many ways like Christ himself, given to the world for the salvation of all people. Thus, God willed that Saint Francis conform to the example of his only son Jesus Christ in his choice of twelve companions, as we have seen, in the wondrous mystery of the Sacred Stigmata, and in his Lenten fasting, which he observed in the following manner.

Having been lodged at the house of a faithful follower near the Lake of Perugia during the time of Carnival, Saint Francis was inspired by God to observe Lent that year on one of the islands in the lake. So Saint Francis asked his devoted son, for the love of God, to take him on Ash Wednesday in his boat to this uninhabited island by night, so that no one might see them, which the man did readily out of the great love and devotion he held toward Saint Francis. Bringing with him only two small loaves of bread, Saint Francis enjoined his friend to tell no one that he was there and to come back for him no sooner than Holy Thursday, at which his friend took leave of the island, leaving Saint Francis there by himself.

As there were no houses on the island to be used as shelter, Saint Francis was content to use a large, thick bush overgrown with vines and plants as a kind of den or hut for himself. There he prayed and contemplated heavenly matters, staying there throughout all of Lent without food or drink, eating no more than half of one of the small loaves he had brought with him, and so his faithful friend found him on Holy Thursday upon his return to the island. Upon seeing a loaf and a half of bread still untouched, he believed that the saint ate the half loaf he did eat out of sheer reverence for the fasting of the blessed Christ, who ate nothing for forty days and forty nights, wishing to follow the example of Christ's fast but setting aside any temptation to vainglory by eating this half loaf of bread as an act of intentional humility.

Afterward, God began to perform miracles in this place where Saint Francis had observed his Lenten abstinence in such a wondrous fashion. People came to this island, building houses and living there, until finally a town grew up, along with a community house for the friars, and all in this place where Saint Francis observed Lent felt great devotion for him and reverence.

Praise be to Jesus Christ and to his poor servant Francis. Amen.

eight

How, on the road with Brother Leo, Saint Francis taught him concerning the things that make for perfect joy. ⤚

The verbal extravagance of this story is the heart of its charm, and the nearly operatic embellishments of Francis's excursus make clear that even as far back as the Middle Ages, Italians were Italians.

⁂

WHILE MAKING THEIR WAY back home to Santa Maria degli Angeli from Perugia one winter, each of them suffering greatly from the extreme cold, Saint Francis called out to Brother Leo walking before him and said, "Brother Leo, even if the Friars Minor were to be known throughout the world as exemplars of holiness and wisdom, please understand—indeed, write it down in words—that such an accomplishment would not make for perfect joy."

Further along in their travels, Saint Francis called out to him a second time, saying, "Oh Brother Leo, even if the Friars Minor were to give sight to the blind, make the crooked straight, drive out demons, restore hearing to the deaf, make the lame to walk and the dumb to speak, indeed, even if they were able to raise the dead to life after four days—write it down in words—such accomplishments would not make for perfect joy."

Still further along the way, Saint Francis shouted out again, "Oh Brother Leo, if the Friars Minor knew all the languages of the world, were possessed of full knowledge of all things, and knew every last word of Scripture so as to prophesy and reveal, not just future things, but every secret in the conscience of every person on earth—write it down in words—even this would not make for perfect joy."

And again, as they continued, Saint Francis called out one more time, in an louder voice, "Oh Brother Leo, little lamb of God, even if the Friars Minor spoke the language of the angels and knew the courses of the stars in the heavens and the powers of every plant, if they were granted insight into every treasure of this world and knew everything there was to know about every bird, fish, or animal, every stone, and every body of water upon the face of the earth, even then—write it down in words—all of this would not make for perfect joy."

A few steps farther, Saint Francis exclaimed, "Oh Brother Leo, even if the Friars Minor knew how to preach so powerfully as to convert every person on earth to a faith in Christ Jesus—write it down—it would not make for perfect joy."

Hearing Saint Francis speak in this way for a good two miles, Brother Leo, with great admiration, finally asked him, "So, holy Father, I beg you to tell me then, on behalf of God, what *would* make for perfect joy?"

Saint Francis replied, "When we have arrived at Santa Maria degli Angeli, drenched in rain, frozen to the bone by the cold, covered in mud, dead with hunger, and when we knock on the door of the house and the doorman comes and asks us, 'Who is there?' and we say, 'We are two of your brothers,' and he answers us saying, 'You liars, you are nothing but a couple of cheating, thieving bandits going about the world stealing alms from the poor, get out of here,' closing the door in our face and sending us out into the wet snow to spend the night cold and hungry—when we then bear such insult, cruelty, and contemptuous treatment with patience, bearing the man no ill will nor saying a single word against him, thinking rather that it was God who led him to speak that way to us, oh Brother Leo—write it down in words—that would make for perfect joy.

"And if we were to knock yet one more time and he were to come to us, angry, swearing at us as if we were nothing but a pair of bothersome louts, driving us away by shouting, 'I told you to get out of here, you worthless thieves, go beg for your bread at the poorhouse. You aren't staying here or getting anything to eat out of us,' and we endure this mistreatment with patience, good cheer, and affection, oh Brother Leo—write it down in words—this makes for perfect joy.

"And if, overcome with hunger and cold, yet one more night we knock and ask for shelter, begging him for the love of God to open up and let us in, and yet a third time, furious, he says, 'I'll give these two obnoxious good-for-nothings what they deserve,' and comes after us with a big, knotted club, throwing us on the ground by our hoods and beating us on the ground in the snow with his club, all of which abuse we endure with patience and good cheer, thinking only of the sufferings of Christ and bearing our own suffering out of love for him, oh Brother Leo—write it down in words—this makes for perfect joy.

"But now, hear the conclusion, Brother Leo. Higher than all the graces and gifts granted by the Holy Spirit to Christ's beloved is the grace of self-mastery, willingly enduring pain, insult, contempt, and discomfort out of love for him. We cannot ourselves glory in any other gift from God, since they are, after all, not our own doing but come from God, as the apostle said, 'What do you have that has not been given to you by God? And even given by God, why do you glory in it, as if it were your own doing?' But, if we endure the cross of our trials and afflictions willingly, in that we can glory, as the apostle has said, 'I will not glory but in the cross of our Lord Jesus Christ.'"

Praise be to Jesus Christ and to his poor servant Francis. Amen.

nine

How Saint Francis tried to teach Brother Leo to speak to him, without success. ⊰⊱

The paradoxes, reversals, and inversions in this tale make it as delightful to read as the previous one, but the most notable feature is how it shows Francis up in his spiritual pride, with humble Leo actually teaching him that mortification is the means, not the end, and that doing God's will—in this case, speaking the truth—is the supreme value.

⚹ ⚹ ⚹

ONCE, IN THE EARLY DAYS of the Order, Saint Francis and Brother Leo found themselves in a place without breviaries to use for praying the Divine Office. So, at the time when Matins was to be recited, Saint Francis said to Brother Leo, "Dear friend, since we have no books to guide us in our prayers, let us take this time to praise God in the following way: I will speak and you will respond to me as I instruct you, in precisely the way that I tell you to, without changing a word. So when I say to you, 'Oh Brother Francis, you have done such evil and committed so many sins in the course of your life that you surely merit damnation to hell,' you, Brother Leo, will answer me by saying, 'Yes, you merit damnation to the deepest, darkest parts of hell, indeed!'" To which Brother Leo, gentle as a dove, replied, "As you wish, holy Father. Let us begin, in the name of the Lord."

Thus, Francis said to him, "Oh Brother Francis, you have done such evil and committed so many sins in the course of your life that you surely merit damnation to hell," to which Brother Leo answered, "Through you God will work such good for so many that surely you will go straight to heaven!"

Saint Francis said, "That's not what you are to say, Brother Leo, please! When I say to you, 'Oh Brother Francis, you have been so wicked and offended God in so many ways, you surely merit damnation to hell,' you are to answer me by saying, 'Yes, you deserve to be consigned to the company of the damned,'" to which Brother Leo once again agreed, "As you wish, holy Father."

Overcome this time with tears, sighing deeply and beating his breast, Saint Francis again said in a loud voice, "Oh Lord of heaven and earth, I have committed so many wicked acts, so many sins against you, that I deserve your eternal damnation," to which Brother Leo replied, "Oh Brother Francis, God will treat you with such mercy that among all the blessed of paradise, you will be especially blessed!"

Wondering why it was that Brother Leo insisted on answering him in the exact opposite way, contrary to his instructions, Saint Francis rebuked him, saying, "Why do you not say what I am asking you to say? I command you, under obedience, to reply to me as I instruct you to. I will say, 'Oh Brother Francis, you wretched sinner, dare you think that God will have mercy on your soul? Given how greatly you have sinned against God the Father of mercy and all consolation, you are not worthy to receive mercy,' to which you, Brother Leo, meek as a lamb, will answer me by saying, 'How true, you are in no way fit to receive God's mercy.'"

So when a third time, Saint Francis said, "Oh Brother Francis, you wretched sinner, dare you think that God will have mercy on your soul? Given how greatly you have sinned against God the Father of mercy and all consolation, you are not worthy to receive mercy," Brother Leo replied, "God the Father Almighty, whose mercy is infinitely greater than your sinfulness, will shower his compassion upon you, and even more, will supply you with every grace."

A gentle anger was kindled in Saint Francis upon hearing this response, and his disturbance showed through his patient demeanor as he reproved Brother Leo a third time, saying, "And precisely why have you presumed to disobey once more? You have said just the opposite of what I wish now many times," to which Brother Leo answered with great humility and reverence, "God knows, holy Father, though I am resolved to do as you wish and answer as you would have me answer you, each time God makes me speak in the way that he wishes, and not as I would wish."

Amazed at this reply, Saint Francis a final time said, "I beg you with my whole heart, please answer me as I tell you to," and Brother Leo agreed once more, "In the name of God, I shall answer you as you wish, I shall!"

Weeping, Saint Francis said, "Wicked Brother Francis, how can you believe that God will have mercy on your worthless soul?" to which Brother Leo replied, "Ah, but God will have mercy on you, and what is more, he will exalt you and glorify you for all eternity, because he has said that 'whoever humbles himself shall be exalted.' I cannot say otherwise, for it is God who speaks through me to you now, holy Father."

Thus, the two passed the night, engaged in this contest of humility, at times in tears, at times greatly consoled, until dawn broke upon them.

Praise be to our Lord Jesus Christ and to his poor servant Francis. Amen.

ten

How Saint Francis made Brother Masseo twirl around
and then sent him to Siena. ⊰

*Public humiliation of various sorts figures greatly into the legends
of Francis and his companions—renouncing family wealth to beg,
dirty and poor, in the street; letting themselves be dragged about
or ridiculed; preaching naked in the pulpit of a church in Assisi;
or, as here, being asked to act like a little child in front of passers-
by. However, Brother Masseo not only takes issue with such
mortifications as these but also has a problem here with Francis's
social manners. These tales illustrate the importance of overcoming
human social convention, for the contemplative life requires a
readiness at all times to do God's will without hesitation or dis-
traction. Francis's inspired knowledge of Masseo's thoughts in
this story and the specific image of twirling certainly allude to the
story in Mark, chapter 9, when Jesus confronts his own disciples
with their secret thoughts concerning who is the greatest among
them and uses the example of a child to make his point that "if
anyone would be first, he must be last of all and servant of all."*

⚹ ⚹ ⚹

ONE DAY, as they were traveling together, Brother Masseo
was a little ways ahead of Saint Francis and came upon the

intersection of three roads, one leading to Florence, the second to Siena, and the third to Arezzo.

"Which road shall we take, Father?" asked Masseo.

"Whichever one God wishes," replied Saint Francis.

"And how do we know which one is God's will?" asked Masseo.

"I'll show you how, right now. Under holy obedience, I command you to stand at the place where these three roads meet and begin to twirl around and around, the way that little children do, and don't stop twirling until I tell you."

So, Brother Masseo did as he was told and began to spin around, and the more he twirled, the dizzier he got, as is usually the case when twirling around like this, until he fell down, but not hearing Saint Francis tell him to stop, and wishing to obey his instruction, he picked himself up and continued twirling faster and faster.

Finally, Saint Francis said, "Good. Stop. Don't move." And so Masseo did, at which Saint Francis asked, "And what road are you facing now?"

Brother Masseo replied, "The road to Siena."

So, Saint Francis said, "Then, that is the road that the Lord wishes us to follow."

Continuing their journey on this road, Brother Masseo couldn't help but wonder why, in front of all those passing by them, Saint Francis had made him twirl around like a little child, but out of respect for his spiritual father, he didn't dare ask why. As they drew close to Siena, the people of that town, having heard of the approach of the saint, came out to greet them, and out of sheer devotion, hoisted the pair of them on their shoulders, not letting any part of them to touch the ground, carrying them to the bishop's residence.

There Saint Francis preached so devoutly, with such holiness, that a wondrous peace and a great spirit of cooperation reigned over all.

Hearing of what Saint Francis had accomplished with his preaching, the bishop of Siena invited him into to stay the night with him in his residence, but the following morning, Saint Francis, humble in all things and seeking only to serve the glory of the Lord, rose early and, without the bishop knowing, went on this way with Masseo, his companion, who began to mutter to himself, "What is this good and holy man doing? First he makes me spin around like a child, and then he leaves the bishop's residence without even a single word of thanks for the hospitality." It seemed to Brother Masseo that Saint Francis was behaving quite rudely, but inspired by the Lord to think better of such inward murmurings, he reproached himself, "Oh Brother Masseo, you are so arrogant, thinking you can stand in judgment of God's action in the world. You are worthy of damnation for your indiscretion and pride. If a veritable angel of Lord had come down and done these deeds himself, he couldn't have done better than Saint Francis yesterday, so if Saint Francis asks you to do even something as silly as throwing stones, you should obey him, for everything he instructs you to do comes directly from the action of God, which is most certainly proven by the fact of the wonderful results that follow. Weren't the fighting townspeople of Siena brought into peaceful harmony with one another, thus sparing many who would have otherwise been victims of violence and bloodshed, or even worse, eternal damnation for their behavior? And yet you, stupid, prideful man, you dare to murmur against the very person through whom God is manifesting his divine will."

Everything Brother Masseo was saying to himself, however, was later revealed by God to Saint Francis, such that Saint Francis eventually turned and said to him, "Pay strict attention to all the thoughts you are entertaining in your heart of hearts at this very moment, brother, for they are inspired by God, and pay no attention to the thoughts you were thinking earlier, for they are the blind, vain, arrogant murmurings inspired by the devil."

With this, Brother Masseo saw clearly that Saint Francis knew all the secrets of his heart, and this confirmed that it was the wisdom of the Lord that inspired all that Saint Francis did.

Praise be to Jesus Christ and to his poor servant Francis. Amen.

eleven

How Saint Francis and Brother Masseo placed the
bread that they had begged on a rock near a fountain,
and Saint Francis praised the virtue of poverty. Then,
Saint Francis prayed to Saint Peter and Saint Paul to
intercede for him with the Lord to inspire him with a
deep love for poverty, and there appeared to him Saint
Peter and Saint Paul. ⤙

*With this tale, Francis's relationship to poverty moves from a mere
means toward spiritual perfection, an instrument he is using to
know God more fully, to something much, much more: a true, full-
fledged, inspired, fire-breathing, visionary love affair; a Franciscan
transfiguration that literally lifts Masseo into the air with near-
erotic abandon and makes possible direct, mystical communication
with Peter and Paul. And as is often the case in these tales, much of
the deepest spiritual teaching is in the small details; in this story we
see Francis and Masseo turn back from their glorious mission to
France and instead bring these stunning revelations and graces—
where?—home, to the everyday place where they were born and live.*

✤ ✤ ✤

THIS WONDERFUL SERVANT and disciple of Christ, holy
father Saint Francis, in order to be conformed in all things to

Christ, followed the example of Christ, who, as the Gospel states, sent his disciples two by two to all the cities and towns where they were needed. In holy obedience, Saint Francis himself first went out into the world and began to preach, and afterward, brought together a group of twelve disciples around himself whom he sent into the world, two by two, likewise, to preach. With various others of his companions assigned to duties elsewhere, Saint Francis took Brother Masseo with him and set out on the road to France. One day, upon reaching a small town, they were very hungry and thus went about, according to the Rule of the Order, begging for their food for the love of God, Saint Francis going to one part of the town, Brother Masseo to the other. But being a man of small stature and of negligible appearance, Saint Francis looked like no more than a street person to those who didn't know who he was and, because of this, he only succeeded in getting few bits of stale bread in the course of the afternoon. On the other hand, because he was taller and much better looking, Brother Masseo received much bigger pieces of bread and even a few small loaves.

Their begging accomplished, the two of them met outside the town to eat their meal beside a beautiful fountain and a large stone, where they each placed what they had received. When Saint Francis saw that what Brother Masseo had managed to get was much more abundant and of better quality than his own meager beggings, he was exceedingly happy and said, "Oh Brother Masseo, we are not worthy of such a treasure," repeating this again and again.

Finally, Brother Masseo asked, "Holy Father, how can you call this a treasure, when we have so little and what little we have here we have begged off the street? Here we are, at dinner, without tablecloths, knives, platters, or bowls, without a house to eat in or even a table to eat on, without servant or maid to wait upon us. What kind of treasure is this?"

To this Saint Francis said, "I call the table we have been set here a treasure because it was set for us not by human hands but rather by the providence of God himself, this wonderful food we have been able to beg, the table of this beautiful stone upon which we are eating, the clear crystal water of this fountain besides us. These treasures lead to me to pray to God that we may learn to love poverty with our whole hearts." And having said these words, they said grace over their meal, refreshed themselves with the bodily food and drink they had been given, and continued on their way to France.

Coming upon a church, Saint Francis said to his friend, "Let us go into this church for a time and pray," and so they did, Saint Francis prostrating himself before the altar in prayer so fervently that the spirit of the Lord came upon him, inspiring his soul with such a fierce love of poverty it appeared that flames of fire were blazing from his face and from out of his mouth. Going toward his companion, still on fire with this divinely inspired love, he exclaimed, "Ah, ah, ah, Brother Masseo, give yourself to me." Three times he said this, and the third time, he lifted Brother Masseo high up into the air with his breath and in a single stroke, cast him down once again, leaving Masseo greatly stunned. Masseo told Saint Francis later what had happened in this church, how he had lifted Masseo into the air with his breath and that in that moment infused Matteo's soul with a sweet consolation of the Holy Spirit such as he had never before experienced in his life. Saint Francis then said to him,

"Dearest friend, let us pray to Saint Peter and Saint Paul and ask them to teach and help us to embrace this immeasurable treasure of poverty, a treasure so worthy, so holy, that we are not worthy to possess it in the miserable vessels of our bodies. So heavenly are its virtues that it teaches us to despise our transient earthly possessions as worthless and continuously acts within us to remove every obstacle that would keep our souls from their progress toward union with God. Poverty is the virtue that enables our souls, while still here on earth, to converse with the angels in heaven. Poverty is the virtue that accompanied Christ to the Cross, that buried him, that raised him from the dead, that ascended with him to heaven, and that grants to every soul that loves it the power to fly to paradise, armed with the virtues of humility and charity. Let's pray, then, to these apostles of the Lord, who so perfectly loved this Gospel pearl of great price themselves, to beg Jesus Christ in his boundless mercy to make us true lovers, faithful followers, and humble disciples of poverty, so precious, so beloved."

Conversing in this manner, they arrived in Rome and went to the church of Saint Peter, where Saint Francis prayed in one small corner and Brother Masseo in another. After a long time in prayer, there appeared to Saint Francis, weeping from devotion, the holy apostles Peter and Paul, in great splendor, and they said, "As you have prayed and longed to observe that which Christ and the holy apostles observed, our Lord Jesus Christ has sent us to announce to you that your prayer has been granted, and that you and your followers will forevermore be perfectly endowed with the gift of holy poverty. And on his behalf, we say to you that whoever perfectly follows your example in this regard will be assured the blessing of eternal life. You and all your followers will be blessed by God." And with these words, the two apostles disappeared, leaving Saint Francis in a state of profound consolation. He arose from his prayer and went to his companion, asking him if God had revealed anything to him, and Masseo said that he had not. So Saint Francis told him how the holy apostles had appeared to him and what they had revealed to him. In their joy, Saint Francis and Brother Masseo decided not to go to France but instead to return to the valley of Spoleto.

Praise be to Jesus Christ and to his poor servant Francis. Amen.

twelve

How God appeared to Saint Francis and his brothers
while they were speaking with him in prayer. ⊷

*The ecstatic mysticism of Francis was always inherent in his
spirituality from the beginning, but while in previous accounts, it
is presented as a private, personal quality of a prayer life carried
out in secret, now, with these stories, it begins to manifest itself
more and more dramatically and, moreover, is shown to be a
communicable spiritual quality. Not only is Francis rapt and
inspired, but he is able to enrapture and inspire others, such that
in the midst of this community whose senses are overcome with
loving union, none other than Christ himself appears. Following
the Franciscan transfiguration now comes the Franciscan
Pentecost.*

⁎⁎⁎

IN THE EARLY DAYS of the Order, Saint Francis had assembled his companions to speak to them of Christ, and seized
with a spirit of fervor, he commanded one of them, in the
name of God, to open his mouth and to speak with God in
whatever way the Holy Spirit inspired him. After he obeyed
this instruction and spoke of God in a wondrous fashion
before them all, Saint Francis asked him to be silent and

turned to another brother, instructing him to do likewise. With similar obedience, this second brother spoke of God with great insight, after which Saint Francis asked him to be silent and instructed a third brother to do the same. This brother spoke of such mystical secrets, with such depth of vision, that Saint Francis could see, with certainty, that his discourse had to be inspired by the Holy Spirit, the clear proof of which was given to them all in the following way: in the midst of their conversation, the blessed Christ himself appeared to them all in the form of a beautiful young man who blessed them and filled them each with such grace and joy that they were taken up in a rapture of spirit and fell to the ground as if dead to the world, only coming back into their senses after considerable time had passed.

"My dearest brothers," said Saint Francis, "Thank God, who has willed for the treasures of divine wisdom to be revealed by the mouths of simple, humble people, God, who opens the mouths of those who cannot speak and teaches the tongues of the simple to speak with great insight."

Praise be to Jesus Christ and his poor servant Francis. Amen.

thirteen

Saint Clare comes to dine with Saint Francis and his
companions at Santa Maria degli Angeli. ⤚

*Part of the perennial charm of this particular story is the self-
conscious use of courtship and wedding imagery on the part of the
narrator, painting these two great saints of the Christian tradition
as a pair of conventionally innocent sweethearts—Francis, like any
naïve young man of the provinces, needing his friends to point out
to him that Clare would like to take their relationship to another
level; their eventual dinner described in minute detail and very
intentionally as a wedding reception, bride and groom beside one
another with best man and maiden of honor at their sides, friends
arranged all around. But then the tale moves quite unexpectedly to
its climax, which combines the romantic and the spiritual, the
erotic and the saintly, in a way typical of the Catholic imagination,
in a single, perfect, practically cinematic image: a blazing fire of
rapture that not only overtakes them but illuminates the entire
countryside.*

⁕⁕⁕

WHEN SAINT FRANCIS was at Assisi, he used to visit Saint
Clare and provide her spiritual direction, such that she
wished, at least once, to have the pleasure of eating with him.

But, though she asked him many times for this, he never granted her this particular consolation, until one day, his companions, seeing how ardently she desired it, said to Saint Francis, "Holy Father, your rigidity on this matter seems to us to be quite at odds with the demands of divine charity. How can you not grant such a small request—simply to share a meal with you—to our sister Clare, holy maiden that she is, and so beloved of the Lord, especially in light of the way that she, in response to your very own preaching, renounced all her wealth and worldly honors? In fact, were she to ask you for an even greater favor than this meager consolation, you would owe it to her to grant it, you who are responsible for her spiritual well-being."

Saint Francis, after some thought, asked them, "So all of you think that I should allow her to come and eat with us?"

They replied, "Yes, Father, we do think it would be the right thing to do, to grant her this grace and consolation."

"Then, if you think it is the right thing to do," said Saint Francis, "so do I. In fact, I believe she would enjoy it even more if we were to invite her to dine with us at Santa Maria degli Angeli. After all, she has been cloistered for quite a long time at San Damiano and it would do her well to come back for a visit to Santa Maria, where she received the veil and became the spouse of Christ. Yes, let us all eat together there, in the name of God the Father."

When the appointed day arrived, Saint Clare left her convent with one of her sisters, and they were joined by some of Saint Francis's companions, who accompanied them to Santa Maria degli Angeli. After saying a prayer before the altar of the Virgin Mary, where she had been shorn and received the habit, they showed her the community house, at which point it was time for dinner. Meanwhile, Saint Francis was preparing the meal on the bare ground, as was his custom, and when it was ready, they had Saint Francis and Saint Clare sit beside one another, flanked by one of his friends, and one of hers, after which the rest of his companions humbly took their places around them.

During the first part of this meal, Saint Francis began to speak of the Lord so sweetly, so gloriously, so wonderfully that an abundance of God's divine grace descended upon all of them, and they were, each of them, enraptured, eyes and hands lifted toward the heavens, such that it appeared to everyone in the surrounding countryside, from Assisi to Bettona, that Santa Maria degli Angeli was on fire, its church and the garden in flames. So real did it seem, in fact, that the inhabitants of Assisi rushed down to the monastery to put out the blaze, only to find Saint Francis and Saint Clare sitting together with all their companions, in a state of holy rapture. It was then that they realized that the fire they were seeing was a fire of the spirit, not a literal fire, and that God had shown them this to reveal how the flame of his divine love burned brightly in the soul of every one of these holy brothers and sisters. With great joy in their hearts and greatly enlightened, the townspeople left and returned to their homes.

After quite a while, Saint Francis, Saint Clare, and their companions came back to their earthly senses, and having been so amply fed by God with food of the spirit, felt little need for the food of this world. Thus, at the end of this blessed meal, Saint Clare and her sister returned to San Damiano and were greeted with happiness by their companions, who had feared that she might have been sent by Saint Francis to found another convent, as he had sent Sister Agnes, Clare's sister, making her abbess of the convent of Monticelli in Florence. For Saint Francis had now and then said to Saint Clare, "Be prepared, for I may need to send you somewhere," to which she, obedient spiritual daughter, replied, "Father, I am always prepared to go wherever you send me." So the sisters of San Damiano rejoiced greatly to see her return that day, and Saint Clare herself felt a profound joy in her own soul as well.

Praise be to Jesus Christ and his poor servant Francis. Amen.

fourteen

How Saint Francis was counseled by Saint Clare and
Brother Silvester that he should go and preach so as
to convert many people, founding the Third Order
but also preaching to the birds and making the
swallows fall silent in wonder. ⤚

*This story is among the most famous episodes in this collection, due
in part to Giotto's classic representation of the scene in the Upper
Basilica of Assisi. However, many might be surprised to find in
reading the original here that this story has practically nothing to
do with some sentimental love of nature on Francis's part. Instead, it
takes great pains to make clear a very different point: namely, the
radical, if not revolutionary, anticlerical stance Francis took with
regard to the church. In discerning his mission, he submits to Clare,
a woman, and after she confirms the Lord's intention for him to go
and preach, the birds that gather around him are very clearly meant
to be emblematic of the laity, a vast, beautiful, varied resource, the
simple, humble people of God to whom Francis has been sent.*

⁎ ⁎ ⁎

FRANCIS, HOLY MAN, humble servant of Christ, shortly
after his own conversion of life, having brought together
many of his companions and received them into the Order,

fell into profound thought and began to question himself and God as to how he ought to proceed. Should he to seclude himself and give himself over to continual private prayer? Or should he go forward now and then to preach in public? Thus, he sought to know God's will on this matter. However, his humility was such that he trusted neither himself nor his own prayerful discernment on such a matter, and instead, he thought it best that God's will be revealed to him through the discernment of others.

For this reason, he called upon Brother Masseo and said, "Go to my good sister Clare and request that she and her spiritual companions pray for me on this matter, that I might be enlightened as to what would be best—am I called to preach or to a life of solitary prayer? Then go to Brother Silvester and request the same of him for me." This Brother Silvester was the man who had earlier, in a vision, seen a cross of gold coming out from the mouth of Saint Francis, a cross as high as the heavens and as wide as the ends of the earth. So devout was Brother Silvester that anything he implored of God was granted, and in his contemplation, he often found himself in direct conversation with God. For all these reasons, therefore, Saint Francis held Silvester in holy esteem.

Brother Masseo went his way, as directed by Saint Francis, first paying a visit to Saint Clare and afterward to Brother Silvester, who upon hearing the request, immediately set himself to praying. In his prayers, he received God's answer: "God says to tell Brother Francis that he did not call him to this way of life for his own good alone but that through it, many souls might bear much fruit on his account and thus be redeemed." Having this answer, Brother Masseo returned to Saint Clare to hear from her the answer to her prayers, and she informed him that, likewise, she and her companions had received the same response as had Brother Silvester.

When Brother Masseo came back to Francis, the holy man received him lovingly, washing his feet and preparing a meal for him, and afterward, called him into the woods. There, in all humbleness of heart, removing his hood, bowing his head and crossing his arms, Francis knelt before Silvester. "What does my Lord Jesus Christ ask that I do?" Brother Masseo replied, "To our Brother Silvester, to our Sister Clare, and to her sisters as well, Christ revealed that it is his will for you to go about the world preaching, since you were not chosen by him for your own good alone but for the spiritual health of others as well." Having therefore heard this answer and by it knowing at last the will of God, Francis got to his feet in a state of great fervor and said, "Then, let us go, in the name of God!" taking with him Brother Masseo and Brother Angelo, both holy men.

Filled with spirit, trusting in God, and with no worry as to destination or path, they arrived at the village of Savurniano where, in preparation for his preaching, he commanded the swallows that were there to cease their twittering and to maintain silence until he was finished. And the swallows obeyed him. There his preaching was so inspiring that all the men and women of the town wanted to leave their homes, abandon their town, and follow him wherever he might go. This Saint Francis could not allow them to do, so he said to them, "Do nothing in haste and by all means, do not leave your homes. I will see to what it is that you must do to maintain your spiritual health." From that time on, therefore, he began to plan a Third Order for laypeople, so as to make redemption available to everyone.

Having consoled them greatly and leaving them well-disposed to a continued amendment of their lives, he went on his way and passed between the towns of Cannara and Bevagno, still in a state of great fervor. While in that place, he raised his eyes at one point and could see a number of trees off the side of the road that were thick with a nearly infinite variety of birds, a great multitude before him. Marveling at the sight of so many of God's creatures, he said to his friends, "Wait for me here in the road as I go to preach the Good News to my little sisters the birds over there." Striking out across the field, he began to preach to the birds, who were on the ground, at which point all the birds in the trees flew down to join them, listening motionless in rapt attention to the holy man, until he concluded his sermon to them and even afterward refusing to leave until he had given each one of them a blessing. So it was, as reported by Brother Masseo to Brother James of Massa, that the holy man Francis went about among the birds, who did not move, touching them with his habit in blessing.

Now, Saint Francis's sermon to the birds was simply this: "Dearest little sisters, you are much beloved by God your Creator, and at all times and in all places you must praise him. He has decreed that you have the freedom to fly anywhere you desire. He preserved your species safe and sound in Noah's ark, so that you and your offspring might survive to this day, and to this day you are beholden to him for the very air that sustains you and that you oversee on his behalf. In addition to these blessings, you neither sow nor reap, and yet God feeds and tends you, provides you with rivers and fountains from which to drink, mountains and valleys in which to take refuge, and tall trees in which to nest. And though you know neither how to spin or to sew, nevertheless God clothes you and your children. He has even given you two and three new sets of clothing each year. Your Creator loves you very much and these many blessings demonstrate his love. So be on your guard, my dearest little sisters, against the sin of ingratitude, and at all times in your lives seek ways to praise the Lord."

After Saint Francis spoke these words to them, all the birds at once opened their beaks, craned their necks, spread their wings, and in reverent gesture, bowed their heads to the ground, showing the holy father in both song and in action just how delighted they were with what he had said to them. Saint Francis took great delight with them and rejoiced, overcome with wonder at how many they were and at their beautiful diversity, at how attentive and affectionate they had been toward him, praising in them God their Creator. When he had finished preaching, Saint Francis made the sign of the Cross over them and bid them to go in peace, at which all the birds flew into the air and broke into ravishing song, creating in flight the very Cross the holy man had just signed them with by dividing themselves into four groups, one group flying toward the east, one toward the west, one south, and one north, and all together singing marvelous songs. Thus they acknowledged how holy Francis—he who bore the marks of the Cross of the Christ on his own body—had come to preach to them and had signed them, too, with the Cross. Accordingly, they flew to the four corners of the earth, a symbol of how renewed devotion to the Cross of Christ throughout the world was due to Saint Francis and his brothers who, like their little sisters, the birds, owned nothing whatsoever and depended solely upon God's providence.

Praise be to Jesus Christ and to Francis in his poverty. Amen.

fifteen

A small boy who entered the Order sees Saint Francis
praying by night and conversing with Christ, the
Virgin Mary, and many other saints. ⫏

*In a cycle of hagiographic stories such as these, it is a mark of the
narrator's skill as a writer to undercut the primary danger of this
genre—an unremitting, and therefore ultimately ineffective, attitude
of hero-worship. The narrator accomplishes this here by placing the
reader's worshipful, almost voyeuristic curiosity about the comings
and goings of Saint Francis into such an utterly believable character
as that of this young boy, who ingeniously attempts to tie himself to
the saint's every move—literally!—and in the end gets more than he
bargained for. By turning the story back on to us, the readers, and
making us look at our own motivations by charming us into an
identification with the naïveté of this child, this tale demonstrates,
once again, the multileveled richness of this collection.*

⚜ ⚜ ⚜

A VERY PURE-HEARTED young boy was received into the
Order while Saint Francis was still living, and the community house in which they lived was so small that they were
forced by necessity to sleep not in beds but on small mats
on the floor. Once, during one of his visits to this house,

following night prayer, Saint Francis went to rest so that he might get up during the night and continue his prayers while all the other brothers were sleeping, as was his custom. This young boy had got it into his head to keep his eye on everything Saint Francis said or did, in part to learn something about the ways of holy men, but mostly just plain curious about what Saint Francis went and did at night when he got up. Just in case he might waver in his resolution and find himself asleep, the young boy decided he would sleep right next to Saint Francis and tie the cord of his habit to that of Saint Francis so that when he would know when Saint Francis got up, which is what he managed to do, without Saint Francis realizing it.

However, that night, while all the other brothers were still sleeping peacefully, Francis went to rise after his rest and found the cord of his habit tied in this way. He gently untied it without waking the young boy and then went out into the woods around the community house to the small monk's cell, where he began his prayers.

A short time later, the young boy awoke to find the cord untied and Saint Francis no longer sleeping beside him, so he got up and went to look for him. Seeing the door to the woods open, he figured that Saint Francis had gone that way and so went into the woods. Coming to the place where Saint Francis was praying, he began to hear the sounds of lively conversation, and coming closer still, he began to see and hear what was going on: a great and marvelous light surrounded Saint Francis, and he could see Christ, the Virgin Mary, and both John the Baptist and John the Evangelist, along with a multitude of angels, all conversing with Saint Francis. The sight and sound of it all stunned the young boy, and he fainted dead away. Some time following this holy apparition, when Saint Francis arose to return to the house, he found the young boy unconscious at his feet, looking as if he had died from sheer fright, and with compassion, Francis bent down, picked him up, and carried him in his arms, just as a good shepherd might carry one of his lambs.

Hearing later about the vision that the boy had witnessed, Saint Francis commanded him to say nothing to anyone about what he had seen, at least as long as Saint Francis was still living, and the young boy, by God's grace and through devotion to Saint Francis, grew into a fine member of the Order. Only after Saint Francis had died did he reveal to his brothers the vision he had seen in his youth.

Praise be to Jesus Christ and to his poor servant Francis. Amen.

sixteen

How the vine at the house of the priest of Rieti was trodden underfoot by the crowds of people who came to see Saint Francis while he prayed there, and yet, how miraculously it produced more wine than ever that year, just as Saint Francis had promised. And how God revealed to Saint Francis that he would enjoy paradise in his turn. ⊰

Like the story of the birds, in which a single image is used to convey multiple meanings, here in this episode the image of the vineyard resonates with a variety of meanings. It suggests a restoration of faith in Christ, the "true vine," as part and parcel of Francis's mission to the Church and to the world; an allusion to the wedding at Cana, itself an allusion to the Eucharist, and the abundance of spiritual fruit always at hand through the experience of faith; not to mention the more obvious and literal aspect of love of God as a form of ecstatic intoxication. Profound insights into the life of faith are conveyed in a few brief strokes by a story that seems on the surface not much more than the account of Saint Francis's visit to Rieti.

✳ ✳ ✳

HEARING THAT SAINT FRANCIS was suffering a serious illness of his eyes, Cardinal Ugolino, protector of the Order, who dearly loved him, wrote that he should come to him in Rieti, where there were excellent eye doctors. Having received this letter from the cardinal, Saint Francis went first to San Damiano to visit Saint Clare, most devoted spouse of Christ, so as to set her soul at ease before he left to go to the cardinal. Once there, however, his eyes worsened until he could see practically nothing, and with him thus unable to leave, Saint Clare made a little cell out of reeds for him so that he could take his rest.

All the same, though, between the pain of his illness and the multitude of rats about the house, Saint Francis found himself completely unable to sleep, either by day or by night, and as his discomfort grew, it occurred to him this pain and tribulation might well be God's punishment upon him for all his sins. So he began to thank God with all his heart, and in a loud voice shouted, "Lord God, I deserve all this and more. Jesus Christ, my Lord, good shepherd, who shows his mercy to us sinners by way of physical pain and bodily afflictions, grant grace and virtue to me, your little lamb, and let neither infirmity nor anguish nor pain separate me from you."

And having prayed in this way, he heard a voice from heaven say, "Francis, answer me. If all the earth were gold, and all the seas and fountains and rivers balm, and all the mountains, hills, and stones gemstones, if you were to find a treasure more precious than all these, more precious than an entire earth made of gold, more precious than every drop of water turned into rare balm, more precious than every mountain and hill transformed into gems, and if you were to be offered this supreme treasure in place of your current affliction, would you not be satisfied with it and rejoice?"

Saint Francis replied, "Lord, I am unworthy of such a treasure."

And the voice of God said once more, "Rejoice, Francis, for eternal life is this treasure which I have set aside and hold in promise for you; and your infirmities and afflictions now are the pledge I give you for this blessed treasure."

So Saint Francis called to his companion, rejoicing over the glorious promise given to him that night, and said, "Let us go to the cardinal," and putting Saint Clare's soul at ease with wise words and humbly taking leave of her, he set out on the road to Rieti.

As Francis drew near to the town, so many people came to see him that he was quite unable to even enter the city and so instead went to pray at a small church a couple of miles outside of town. Hearing that he had gone to that church to pray, the townsfolk who wanted to see him followed him there as well, trampling the vineyard around the church and knocking all the grapes off the vines.

The priest of the church, seeing what they had done to his vines, was very upset and regretted having allowed Saint Francis to come to the church at all. God revealed to Saint Francis what was in the mind of this priest, and Francis brought him close and said, "Dearest father, how many barrels of wine does this vineyard produce in a good year?"

"In a good year," said the priest, "twelve or so."

Saint Francis replied, "So I ask you, father, to endure with patience my staying with you for these few days, for I find it quite restful here, and I further ask, for the love of God and for his poor servant, let all those who would gather the grapes from your vines to do so. I promise you, by Christ Jesus my Lord, that your vines will produce twenty barrels this year."

And thus, Saint Francis stayed there for a time, seeing a great fruitfulness of spirit in the many souls that came to see him, growing intoxicated on the wine of divine love they drunk with him and thus renouncing the world, and the priest had faith in Saint Francis's promise to him, so he left the vineyard open to all who came.

Miracle of miracles! Though the vineyard was ruined and only a few clusters of grapes here and there were left, when the time of harvest came, the priest gathered what little he could find, putting the bits and pieces into the wine press, and just as Saint Francis had promised, twenty fine barrels of wine were produced that year. Clearly the miracle is meant to show that just as a vineyard trampled and spoiled can, by the merits of Saint Francis, abound in wine, so, too, may Christians, deprived of virtue by their own sinfulness, abound in the fruit of a conversion of life as well, through the merits of Saint Francis.

Praise be to Jesus Christ and to his poor servant Francis. Amen.

seventeen

One of Saint Francis's holiest of miracles, taming the fierce wolf of Gubbio. ⤛

This tale rivals anything one might find in the Gospels for its endless breadth of possible interpretation. But whatever any of us might read into the figure of the wolf—innate human aggressiveness, selfishness, our hopeless propensity to violence, inability to love neighbor as oneself, mimetic rivalry—what is indisputable is what Francis reveals to the townspeople and to us: that compassion requires courage for it to become an agent of true transformation, and where courage and compassion are brought to bear, defensiveness, poverty, and enmity can be turned into cooperation, abundance, and familiarity.

⁎⁎⁎

Dᴜʀɪɴɢ ᴛʜᴇ ᴛɪᴍᴇ that Saint Francis lived in the town of Gubbio, there was in the town a large wolf, ferocious in behavior and terrible in appearance, who preyed not only upon the animals of the town but upon the townspeople as well. For this reason, they were greatly afraid of the wolf, and thus went about heavily armed at all times, lest they came upon it. Nevertheless, for all their precautions, any one who met the wolf alone was defenseless, such that after a time no one dared to venture outside the town at all.

Feeling great compassion for the people of Gubbio, Saint Francis decided to go out of the town and meet the wolf, which the townsfolk of course discouraged him from doing. But, making the sign of the Cross and placing all his trust in God, he left the town with his companions who, after a time, seized by fear themselves, refused to go any farther and left Saint Francis to meet the wolf on the road by himself.

Now many of the townspeople, wishing to see a miracle, followed at some distance behind Saint Francis. The wolf, seeing this great crowd, leapt forward toward Saint Francis, jaws wide open, but Saint Francis stepped toward him and made the sign of the Cross, calling out to him, "Come here, Brother Wolf. In Christ I command you to do no harm to me nor to anyone else." What a wonder to recount! As soon as Saint Francis made the sign of the Cross, the ferocious wolf stopped in its tracks, closed its jaws, and became as gentle as a lamb, curling up at his feet.

Saint Francis spoke to it, saying, "Now, Brother Wolf, you have caused a lot of harm around here and have done some very evil things, hurting and killing God's creatures without permission; and not only God's animals, but you have even dared to kill human beings, who were made in the image of God. For this, by all rights, you deserve to be hanged, like a thief or a murderer. Everyone curses you and says all manner of things against you, and the whole of this town is your enemy. But, Brother Wolf, I wish to make peace between you and your enemies, so that you no longer do them harm, so that they might forgive you all the evil you have done in the past, so that you no longer need to be hunted by men and dogs." As he spoke, the wolf nodded his head in understanding of all Saint Francis was saying, his body, tail, and ears completely attentive to everything Saint Francis did.

Further, Saint Francis said, "Brother Wolf, on my part, so that you keep the peace here in town, I promise you that I will see that, for the rest of your life, you are provided for by the townsfolk, so that you will never go hungry again, for I know that it is due to hunger that you have caused the harm you have caused. If I grant you this then, Brother Wolf, will you promise me now never again to harm any human being or animal? Is that a promise?" And once again the wolf nodded as a sign of his promise.

Saint Francis concluded then by saying, "Brother Wolf, I would like you to give me a pledge of your promise, so that I might have faith in it," extending his hand to receive this pledge of faith from the wolf, who raised his right paw and placed it upon Saint Francis's hand, giving him his solemn pledge.

"Brother Wolf," said Saint Francis, "I command you, in the name of Christ Jesus, to trust me completely and to come with me now to seal this peace in the name of God." Obediently the wolf went with him, following him as a little lamb would, to the great astonishment of the townspeople, who spread the news of this happening far and wide throughout the city such that everyone, man, woman, short, tall, young and old, all came to the town square to see the wolf with Saint Francis.

With the whole of the town before him, Saint Francis went up and began to preach to them, telling them, among other things, how for our sins God allows plagues and other evil things to occur, but that the fires of hell are far more dangerous and last an eternity for those who are damned—unlike the rage of a mere wolf who can only kill our bodies. "How much more than the mouth of a mere animal should we fear the raging mouth of hell itself? Change your lives, my dear friends, turn to God and renounce your own evil ways. God will deliver you from the wolf of your present life and from the fires of hell in the life to come."

Finishing his sermon, Saint Francis then said, "Listen, my brothers and sisters: our Brother Wolf here before you has given me his promise and a pledge of his faith, that he has made his peace with you all and will no longer do you any harm, for which you are to give him all that he needs. I stand here as guarantee that he will observe the peace he has pledged."

The whole town answered by promising that they would indeed make sure the wolf was always well fed, and before them, Saint Francis turned to the wolf and said, "And you, Brother Wolf, do you promise to observe this covenant of peace and to do no harm to human beings, animals, or any living creature?"

The wolf knelt before him and, with gentle gestures of his body, tail, and ears, nodded his head, giving sign as he could of his promise to keep this covenant.

Saint Francis then said, "Brother Wolf, I wish for you to give me once more a pledge of your promise, as you did earlier outside of town, here now before all the townspeople so that you will not betray your promise nor my guarantee of you to them." So the wolf raised his right paw and placed it in Saint Francis's hand, at which the townspeople marveled and rejoiced, as much out of devotion to Saint Francis as for the novelty of the miracle they had witnessed and the peaceful demeanor of the wolf. Raising their voices to heaven, they praised and blessed God for having sent them Saint Francis, who through his merits had delivered them from the mouth of this cruel beast.

For two more years the wolf lived among them in Gubbio and went about from door to door, as a friend to all, harming no one and without being harmed in any way himself, being given food to eat by one and all, without even so much as a dog barking at him, until, at the end of the two years, he died of old age. The people of Gubbio were much grieved by his passing, for they had grown used to his gentle presence in the town, which reminded them at all times of the virtue and sanctity of Saint Francis.

Praise be to Jesus Christ and to his poor servant Francis. Amen.

eighteen

How Saint Francis tamed wild turtledoves. ⊰

The tales of the birds and the wolf in previous stories are less about Saint Francis as a spiritually besotted "nature boy" than they are powerful representations of certain spiritual states. So, too, here: the poor, feckless turtledoves described here, ransomed with gentleness and love, are meant to be symbols of innocence and passivity in the spiritual life, illustrated best by Saint Francis himself who speaks to them as his "little sisters."

⁕ ⁕ ⁕

A YOUNG MAN who had caught a great number of turtledoves was taking them to market when he crossed paths with Saint Francis, who had always felt a great compassion in his heart for these gentle animals. Casting a merciful eye toward the turtledoves, he said to the young man, "Be a good boy, and let me have those birds, would you? Doves are such sweet little animals that Holy Scripture likens them to the faithful, pure, and humble among us. I would hate to see them fall into the cruel hands of those who would put them to death." Without a thought, inspired by God, the young man handed them all to Saint Francis. Holding them close to his chest, Saint Francis began to speak to them softly, "Oh my dear little sisters, so simple, so innocent, so pure, why did you let yourselves be taken like this? I will now see to it that you escape the fate of death and will have, each of you, your own little nest, so you can be fruitful and multiply, as the Creator has commanded you to do."

And so Saint Francis did, making nests for them, where, some time later, in front of the brothers, they began to lay their eggs and hatch them, going about with Saint Francis and the other brothers as tamely as a brood of hens that had been raised by them. Nor did they ever leave the brothers, even when Saint Francis gave them his blessing and bid them to depart.

To the young man who had given the turtledoves to him, Saint Francis sad, "My young man, you will be a brother in this Order and you will graciously serve Jesus Christ." And so it was that the young man became a friar and lived a holy life in the Order.

Praise be to Jesus Christ and his poor servant Francis. Amen.

nineteen

Saint Francis converted the sultan of Babylon and the prostitute who tempted him to sin. ⤙

While the rest of Christendom is shipping off to the Holy Land on armed Crusades to militarily subdue the "infidel," this story presents the Franciscan counterresponse to such misguided action: a true follower of Christ the Crucified desires not conquest but the self-abnegation of martyrdom. Conversion, Francis shows us, is not about force or victory but about the opposite, the mastering of passion—hence the inclusion in the middle of this story of what might otherwise seem to be an irrelevant erotic interlude—and the result is an exemplary life of integrity shared with others in true, open relationship. In our post-9/11 world, the person of Francis, in his imitation of Jesus here, delivers a message more relevant than ever.

⤙⤙⤙

SAINT FRANCIS, filled with zeal for the Christian faith and a longing for martyrdom, set out to sea with twelve of his holiest companions to visit the sultan of Babylon. Upon reaching one of the provinces held by the Saracens, he found that all the roads were being guarded by ruthless men, so that no Christian could pass that way without being killed. However, it pleased God that they not be killed, but instead were captured, beaten, bound, and taken before the sultan, where, instructed by the Holy Spirit, Saint Francis began to preach of the faith of Christ Jesus with such divine inspiration that he was ready to be burned at the stake for that faith, if it were God's will. Thus it was that the sultan became quite devoted to Saint Francis, impressed by the constancy of his faith, by his disdain for the things of this world—for Francis refused any and every gift that the sultan offered him, out of love for poverty—and by his fervent desire for martyrdom. From that time forward, then, the sultan willingly listened to whatever Saint Francis said and often called for him, allowing him and his companions to preach wherever they wished throughout the province, giving that as token of his protection, so that no one would harm them.

Having been given such license, Saint Francis sent his companions out in pairs to preach the Christian faith in all the various parts of the province, and he went himself with one of them to a certain region where they took their rest at an inn. It so happened that also at this inn was a woman of beautiful appearance but of debauched character who took it upon herself, wicked woman, to tempt Saint Francis into sin.

"Yes, then," said Saint Francis to her invitation, "Yes. Let's sleep together." So, she brought him to her room, whereupon Saint Francis said, "Please, come with me. I shall show you an even better bed," and she went with him to the great hearth in the center of the inn where there was a blazing fire. Fervently inspired, he undressed before her and threw himself into the middle of the hearth, in the midst of the fire, inviting her to do likewise, to undress and join him in this blazing, beautiful bed. Seeing him stand there, face radiant with happiness, neither burned nor even slightly singed, the woman felt a deep fear of God and a great compunction burning in her heart. Having witnessed this miracle, she not only repented of her evil ways and wicked intention but was completely and wholly converted to faith in Christ and became a woman of such great sanctity that she saved many souls throughout the region.

After a time, seeing that he had fulfilled his mission in this part of the world, it was revealed to him by God that he should return with his companions to the land of the faithful. Gathering them all together once again, Saint Francis went to the sultan to take his leave. "Brother Francis," said the sultan, "I would willingly convert to the Christian faith, but I fear doing so right now, for, should my people hear of such a thing, they might well kill me, along with you and all your companions, and since I believe you still have much good to do and I likewise have many affairs of great importance to bring to conclusion, I would not like to be the cause of your death nor mine. However, tell me now how I might be saved, for I am prepared to do whatever you tell me."

So, Saint Francis said to him, "My lord, I will be taking my leave of you now, but once I am back in my homeland and have gone to heaven, by the grace of God, after my death, if the Lord so wills it, I will send two of my friars to you, from whom you shall receive baptism in Christ, and thus you will have salvation, as it has been revealed to me from Jesus Christ our Lord. In the meantime, free yourself of every obstacle, so that when God's grace does come to you, you will be prepared to live a life of faith and devotion." The sultan promised to do so.

With that, Saint Francis returned home in the estimable company of his holy friends, and after a number of years,

Saint Francis gave up his soul to God in death. The ailing sultan, believing in the promise Saint Francis had made him, sent men to guard the roads and commanded them that, should they see friars dressed in the habit of Saint Francis, they were to bring them to him right away.

Indeed, Saint Francis did appear to two of the brothers and ordered them to go without delay to the sultan and ensure the salvation of his soul, as he had promised. They set out to sea, arrived in the sultan's land, and were taken quickly to him, where, upon seeing them, the sultan rejoiced greatly and said, "Now I truly know that, for my salvation, God has sent me his servants, according to the promise that Saint Francis, by divine revelation, had made to me many years ago." After receiving instruction in the Christian faith and being baptized by the two friars, he was given new life in Christ, and though dying of the illness from which he was suffering, his soul had been saved by the merits and prayers of Saint Francis.

twenty

How Saint Francis miraculously healed a leper, body and soul, and what the leper's soul said to him on his way to heaven. ◄◄

With this story of a leper's healing, the life of Francis is placed within the rich and ancient Judeo-Christian Biblical tradition that has used leprosy as a religious and spiritual symbol in a variety of ways: to reflect on the nature and purpose of social exclusion or inclusion; to represent punishment for sin; to express concern for spiritual purity and fear of impurity and contagion; to signify death and rebirth; and to identify the body as a boundary between the visible, outward self and the inner, perhaps truer, Self. Notable in this story is the physical intimacy with which Francis undertakes the healing action, much like Christ himself in the Gospels, unafraid of direct, physical contact with those seen as unhealthy or frightening. Likewise, by addressing the man's underlying spiritual state before restoring him to physical health, Francis demonstrates with his compassion how we might hold our suffering in a way that is beneficial, rather than destructive, to ourselves and to others.

⁂

THAT TRUE DISCIPLE OF CHRIST, Saint Francis, throughout the many trials he suffered in his life, tried with all might to follow Christ, the perfect teacher. Thus, he often was able, through divine action, to heal both the body and the soul of a person, as has been written of Christ. Not only, therefore, did he willingly tend to lepers himself, but furthermore instructed the friars of his Order, wherever they found themselves, to likewise tend to the needs of lepers out of love for Christ, who was himself willing to be treated as a leper for our sake.

So it happened one day that, near a place where Saint Francis was staying, the friars were working in a hospital for those sick with leprosy, in which there was one leper so unbearably impatient and ill-mannered that everyone believed him to be possessed by a demon. He would hit and swear at anyone who tried to attend to him, but worse still, he cursed Christ and his blessed Mother, the Virgin Mary, and his behavior was such that no one was able to tend to him. Now, while the brothers were able, for their own part, to patiently bear the insults and contempt he heaped on them so as to grow in the virtue of patience, they were quite unable to bear hearing the blasphemies this man would utter against Christ and the Blessed Mother. And so, in the end, they decided to leave this leper to his own devices, unattended, but only after informing Saint Francis of their decision.

Saint Francis, who was staying nearby, went to this unbalanced leper and upon seeing him, greeted him by saying, "May God grant you peace, dearest brother."

The leper answered him, "What peace can I get from God, who has taken all peace and everything I had in this world away from me and left me here, stinking and rotten?"

Saint Francis said, "My son, be patient. Bodily ills are given to us in this world for the good of our souls, and they can be of great spiritual benefit to us, if they are borne with patience."

The sick man replied, "And how can I bear this continual pain that afflicts me day and night? Not only am I afflicted by this horrid illness but, what is worse, the friars you sent to help me are not tending to me as they should." From this, it was revealed to Saint Francis that indeed this leper was possessed by an evil spirit, and so he went and began to pray to God for him in earnest.

Having thus prayed, he came back to him and said, "My son, I will tend to you from now on, since you are so unhappy with all the others."

The leper said, "Very good! But what can you do for me that the others cannot?"

Saint Francis said, "Whatever you wish, I shall do."

The leper said, "I want you to wash me from head to toe, for I stink so badly that I cannot even stand it myself."

So Saint Francis went quickly, prepared some warm water with sweet-smelling herbs, undressed the man, and began to wash him with his own bare hands as another brother poured the water over him, and miraculously, wherever Saint Francis placed his hands, the leprosy was removed and the man's skin was healed. Moreover, just as the skin was healed, so, too, did the man's soul begin to heal. In seeing himself returned to health, he began to feel a deep compunction and repented of his sins, weeping bitterly, almost as if he was being cleansed of his sins through his contrition and tears in the same way he was being cleansed of his leprosy by the washing of the water.

Having been completely healed, body and soul, he humbly confessed his sins, crying out loud, "Woe to me, I deserve to be damned to hell for the way I have cursed and insulted the friars, for my impatience and for all the many blasphemies I have uttered against God." And for fifteen days, he wept bitterly of his sins and begged for God's mercy, making a general confession to a priest.

Saint Francis, having seen this miracle accomplished by God at his hand, thanked the Lord and departed, traveling far away from that place, for out of humility, he wished to eschew any glory of his own and sought through all that he did to render glory and honor to God alone.

However, it was God's will that, after fifteen days of penitence, this same leper fell ill with yet another physical affliction, and comforted by the Sacraments of the church, he died a holy death. His soul, on its way to heaven, appeared in the air before Saint Francis, who was in the forest deep in prayer, and said to him, "Do you know who I am?"

Saint Francis said, "No. Who are you?"

"I am the leper that the blessed Lord Jesus Christ healed by your merits, and now I am going to life eternal, for which I give thanks to God and to you. May you be blessed in body and soul, and may God bless your words and your deeds. Through you, many souls of this world will be saved. And know that not a single day will pass when the angels and saints will not thank God for the blessings that have come to fruition through you and your Order throughout the world. Take heart, then, and give thanks to God, and may you be blessed." Having said these things, his soul went up to heaven, and Saint Francis was deeply consoled.

Praise be to Jesus Christ and to his poor servant Francis. Amen.

twenty-one

How Saint Francis converted three murderous thieves
and made them friars; and the most exalted vision
given to one of them, who was a very saintly friar. ⤙

*This story continues the theme begun first with the wolf of Gubbio
and further elaborated in the healing of the leper. What some among
the "righteous" reject as violent, antisocial behavior on the part of
others and respond to with fear and loathing, Francis repeatedly and
consistently sees as a symptom of underlying physical or spiritual
lack, which he, and his followers, are called to fill with humble,
courageous, compassionate, generous service, both literally and
spiritually. Conversion is not a matter of changed intellectual belief
but rather a process of being brought back into human community
through nourishment, companionship, and teaching. The second
part of this story repeats this theme in more symbolic form, using
classic medieval images of purgatory within the friar's dream to
illustrate further how conversion is not a quick and easy adoption
of spiritual purity but rather a slow and arduous task of humility,
patience, and detachment.*

⁂

ONCE, WHILE SAINT FRANCIS was traveling through the
wilderness of Borgo San Sepolcro, he passed by a castle called

Monte Casale, and a well-dressed young nobleman came to him, saying, "Holy Father, I very much wish to become a friar with you."

Saint Francis replied, "My son, you are young, quite noble, and very refined. I think that you might not be able to bear the poverty and ascetic way that we live."

The nobleman said in response, "But Father, are you not mortal men like myself? Just as you are able to bear such demands, so, too, shall I, with the grace of Christ."

Saint Francis was very pleased with this answer to him and so, blessing the young man, received him into the Order and gave him the name Brother Angelo, which fit him well, and shortly afterward, Saint Francis made him the guardian of their community house in Monte Casale.

Now, during that time there were, in the region, three notorious thieves going about, doing much evil to the people, one of whom came one day to the community house and begged Brother Angelo to give him something to eat. The guardian, however, took this opportunity to reproach him in the strongest way, answering him, "You are heartless, murderous thieves who shamelessly steal the fruits of others' labor and now you come here, impudent and full of presumption, to devour the alms that have been sent by God to feed his servants. You don't deserve to be walking on this earth, you who have no reverence for your fellow men nor to the Lord who created you. Go about your misbegotten business, thief, and don't come back here again."

At that moment, Saint Francis returned to the house from his begging, with a loaf of bread and a flask of wine in his sack that he and his companions had been given, and when the guardian recounted to him what he had said and done,

Saint Francis took great issue with it, saying that it was he, the guardian, who had behaved in a heartless way. Saint Francis said, "More people are brought to God through kindness than through harsh reproaches. Our master and teacher Jesus Christ, whose Gospel we have vowed to observe, tells us that the healthy have no need of a physician but those who are ill, and that he came not to call the righteous but to call sinners to repentance, which is the reason he so often sat at table with them. Thus, you have acted contrary to the demands of charity and to the Gospel of our Lord Jesus Christ, and I order you under holy obedience to take this loaf of bread and flask of wine and seek high and low, through all the hills and the valleys, for these thieves until you find them, and when you do, give them this bread and wine for me. And further, kneel before them and humbly ask forgiveness for the cruelty you have shown them. Then, ask them, for me, to stop their wrongdoing and to start living out of love for God and neighbor. If they promise to do this, tell them that I promise on my part to make sure all their needs are provided for and that they will always have food and drink. When you have done and said all these things, then you may return here in humility." While the guardian was following Saint Francis's instructions, Saint Francis began to pray that the Lord would soften the hearts of the thieves and that they would be converted to repent of their evil.

The obedient guardian eventually did find the thieves, gave them the bread and wine from Saint Francis, and accomplished all that Saint Francis had instructed him to say and do. And as they ate the alms of Saint Francis, they began to reflect to themselves, saying, "Woe is us, miserable sinners that we have been. How harsh the punishments of hell will be for us, we who have gone about stealing from our neighbors, beating them, hurting them, even killing them. And for all these evil and wicked acts we have committed, we don't feel remorse in our conscience nor even fear of the Lord. And now here is this saintly friar, who has come to us, begging our forgiveness for a few mean words he had every right to speak to us earlier, humbling confessing his sin to us and, what's more, giving us bread and wine, with a generous promise of even more from his own spiritual father. Truly these friars are saints, worthy of paradise, whereas we are sons of eternal perdition, who surely deserve the fires of hell, and who each day merit further damnation. How can we possibly earn God's mercy for all the sins we have committed?"

These and similar words they spoke one to another, saying in turn, "Yes, all this is true, but what can we do now?" until one of them said, "Let's go to Saint Francis himself, and if he assures us that it is possible to be received back into the grace of God after all our sins, then let us do whatever he tells us so that we can avoid damning our souls to hell for all eternity."

Agreeing to this course of action, the three of them hurriedly made their way to Saint Francis and said, "Holy Father, in light of all the wicked and sinful deeds we have done, we do not believe that we can be received back into the grace of God. But if you hold any hope whatsoever that it might be possible for God to show us his grace, we are prepared to do whatever you tell us to and to do penance as you instruct."

Saint Francis took them to himself, showed them great love and kindness, spoke of so many examples of God's grace and forgiveness that they began to believe God would be merciful to them, and promised them that he himself would pray to

God on their behalf, for God's mercy is infinite. "Even if our own sins are infinite, God's mercy, the Gospel tells us, is still more infinite. For Saint Paul writes, 'Christ came into this world to redeem sinners.'"

And so, through this instruction and these words, the three thieves renounced the Devil and all his ways and Saint Francis received them into the Order, whereupon they began to do penance for their sins. Two of the three died shortly after their conversion and went to heaven, but the third lived a life of continual penance for fifteen years, fasting three days a week in addition to the communal fasts that he observed with his brothers, going about barefoot and clad in a thin tunic, and never going back to sleep after Matins.

It was at this time that Saint Francis passed from this earthly life into the next, and this particular brother, having now spent many years in continual penance, one night, after Matins, was strongly tempted to sleep, so strongly that he could not resist and maintain his vigil as he was used to doing. So he took himself to bed, but the moment he laid his head down to sleep, he became enraptured and his spirit was led up to the peak of a high mountain to the edge of a steep cliff where broken rocks and sharp stones covered the hillside, a fearsome sight to behold. Then the angel who had led him to this place pushed him off the cliff and down the hillside, where he fell upon all the sharp stones. The friar landed at the bottom, his body shattered to pieces, whereupon the angel came to him as he lay on the ground and said, "Arise. You have a great journey ahead of you."

The friar replied, "You are a cruel and unreasonable man, pushing me off this cliff to die here, shattered, and now saying to me, 'Arise.'"

The angel then came to him, touched him and restored his shattered body to perfect health, and then led him to a broad plain filled with thorny plants, thistles, and brambles, which the angel said he must cross barefoot until he reached the other side, where a fiery furnace was blazing, into which he should enter.

When the friar had crossed this great plain, in agony and pain, the angel said, "Go into the fire, as you have been commanded."

The friar replied, "You are a heartless guide. I am practically dead from the agony of crossing the plain and now, for my reward, I am to throw myself into this fire?" Looking into the furnace, he could see many demons with iron pitchforks in their hands and he hesitated to go in, but the demons skewered him with their forks and pulled him into the fire.

From within the flames, he saw one of his former companions, on fire from head to toe, and so asked him, "Oh my poor, unfortunate friend, how is it that you have ended up here?"

He answered, "Continue on a bit and you will find my wife, who shall tell you the cause of my damnation."

The friar continued onward and did find the man's wife, covered in flames, buried in a pile of grain also in flames, and he asked her, "Oh miserable and unfortunate woman, what have you done to deserve such torment?"

She answered, saying, "During the great famine that Saint Francis had predicted, my husband and I cheated our customers of the grain they bought from us, falsifying the measures, and now I am burning in all the grain that we stole from them."

And with these words, the angel pushed the friar out of the

furnace and said, "Prepare to embark upon a horrible journey that you now must make."

Full of sorrow, he said, "Stern guide that you are, do you feel any compassion for me? I am burned all over from the furnace and now you wish to take me on a dangerous and horrible journey?"

So the angel touched him and healed him of his burns, and led him to a bridge, very narrow, fragile, and slippery, unsupported on either bank, over a terrible river, reeking of dragons, snakes, and scorpions.

The angel said to him, "Cross this bridge. Yes, you must cross this bridge."

The friar replied, "How can I cross this bridge without falling into this terrible river?"

The angel said, "Follow me and place your foot wherever I place mine, and in this way, you will make your way across."

So the friar followed in the footsteps of the angel, as he had been told to do, and made it to the middle of the bridge, whereupon the angel flew away to a high mountaintop, where the friar could see him. The friar was now without a guide and, looking downward, he could see the terrible animals below him, heads above the water, jaws wide open, ready to devour him should he fall. Shaking with terror, he did not know what to do, whether to turn back or to go forward.

Overcome with tribulation of spirit and having only God in which to take refuge, he bent down and held on to the bridge, and with all his heart, weeping great tears, he called upon God in his great mercy to save him. Having prayed thus, he suddenly felt himself grow wings and, rejoicing in this, he decided to wait until the wings grew large enough to let him fly from the bridge up to where the angel was standing. But after some time, feeling a strong desire to get off this bridge, he began to fly, but because his wings had not yet grown large enough, he fell back down onto the bridge and the wings lost their feathers.

So once more, he gripped the bridge and prayed to the Lord, and after his prayers, he felt wings growing yet again, but, as he had the first time, he did not wait until they were perfectly formed and instead tried to take flight too early, whereupon he fell back down onto the bridge and lost the feathers a second time.

Seeing that the problem was his impatience and that were he to try to fly too soon, he would merely fall back down again, he said to himself, "Now, if the wings grow back a third time, I will wait until they are big enough so that can fly without falling back down to earth." And thinking these thoughts, he felt the wings growing back a third time, and this time he waited until they had grown very, very large, such a long time that it seemed to him that he had been waiting 150 years. Finally, a third time he arose, and with all his strength, he flew up to the place where the angel had flown, which looked like the house of a religious community.

The friar knocked on a door that the angel had entered, and a doorman answered, saying, "Who are you who have come here?"

The friar replied, "I am one of the Friars Minor."

The doorman said, "Wait here and let me get Saint Francis to come and take a look and see if he recognizes you." While he was gone, the friar began to look at the wondrous walls of the house, infused as they were with light, so clear and transparent that he was able to see choirs of saints beyond them, and as he stood there, stunned by their beauty, there came to him Saint Francis, Brother Bernardo, and Brother Giles. Following Saint Francis was a multitude of holy men and women who had followed his way of life, so many that they seemed beyond number. And when Saint Francis had reached where he stood, he said to the doorman, "Let him enter. He is indeed one of my friars."

As soon as he entered the house, he felt such a deep sense of spiritual peace, and such a sweetness pervaded his soul, that all the trials he had been through were instantly forgotten, almost as if they had never happened.

Saint Francis took him around inside, showing him many wonderful things and saying, "My son, you must return to the world for seven more days, during which you are to prepare yourself with great devotion, for at the end of those seven days, I will come for you and will bring you back here with me, to the house of the blessed." Saint Francis was wearing a wondrous cloak, adorned with beautiful stars, and the five wounds of his stigmata shown forth splendidly as if they, too, were beautiful stars, illuminating the entire house with their light. Brother Bernardo wore a crown of beautiful stars as well, and Brother Giles was surrounded with a marvelous brilliance, and along with them, many other holy friars whom he had not known in the world. Taking his leave of Saint Francis, the friar returned, with some reluctance, to the world.

Upon awakening, he came back to his senses and heard the friars singing Prime, that is, morning prayer, by which he realized that the vision merely had lasted from Matins to Prime, though it had seemed to him that many years had passed. He recounted to the guardian all that had occurred in his vision, and on the seventh day, he fell ill with a fever. On the eighth day, Saint Francis came to him, as he had promised, with a great multitude of glorious saints, taking his soul with them to the kingdom of the blessed in life eternal.

Praise be to Jesus Christ and his poor servant Saint Francis. Amen.

twenty-two

How the Evil One, many times in the form of the Crucified Christ, appeared to Brother Ruffino, telling him that all the good he had done was for naught, since he was not among those chosen for eternal life, but how Saint Francis, by way of revelation, came to know this and showed Brother Ruffino how it was not true and that he had been mistaken in believing it. ⤙

Francis's experience of the talking crucifix in San Damiano, a principal turning point in his own religious conversion, is here turned on its head, making this story with its paradoxical inversion one more masterful discourse on the dangers of spiritual pride. Who cannot see themselves in Ruffino, full of good and pious intentions but secretly not truly willing to let God be God and to admit his own limitations, deciding in the isolation of his own mind whether he has been saved or damned, so that he, and not the Most High, remains firmly, clearly in control? And what better—or more shockingly earthy—image of detachment than that of defecation to accomplish the discernment that is necessary? When we have emptied ourselves out completely, the story seems to say, only then is a true discernment of spirits possible.

⁎⁎⁎

Brother Ruffino, one of the finest noblemen of Assisi and a companion of Saint Francis, was a man of considerable holiness, and yet found himself frequently besieged by the demon of doubt concerning predestination, such that his soul was often troubled, and he went about life depressed and sad. This particular demon put it into his head that he was not among the number of the elect predestined for eternal life and consequently would be damned to eternal hellfire, so that whatever service he rendered in the Order was useless effort. As the temptations of this doubt grew day by day, Brother Ruffino grew ever more ashamed to reveal these thoughts of his heart to Saint Francis, though he never missed prayer and participated in all the usual fasts.

The Evil One began to drag Brother Ruffino further and further into sadness and began to attack him, along with his interior battles, with all manner of false visions as well, one day actually coming to him in the form of a crucifix and saying, "Oh Brother Ruffino, why are you tormenting yourself with such prayers and penances, since you are not among those predestined for eternal life? Believe me, I know whom I have elected and predestined, and pay no attention to Pietro Bernardoni's son if he should tell you something different. In fact, do not even discuss this matter with him, for neither he nor anyone else truly knows except for me, for I am the Son of God. And I am telling you, you are most certainly among the damned, along with that son of Pietro Bernadoni, your own father, and even his father, likewise—all of them, damned. Whoever tells you different is deceiving you." Having heard such words, Brother Ruffino felt himself slowly overcome with a spiritual darkness such that he lost all the faith and love that he had once felt for Saint Francis, telling him nothing about what was transpiring within him.

However, what Brother Ruffino did not tell Saint Francis, the Holy Spirit revealed instead, and seeing in a vision the great danger that his friar was suffering, Saint Francis sent Brother Masseo to get him and to bring him to Saint Francis. But Brother Ruffino said to Masseo gruffly, "I have no business with Brother Francis."

Brother Masseo, filled with divine wisdom, perceived the deception wrought by the Devil and said, "Oh Brother Ruffino, surely you know that Brother Francis is like an angel of God who has enlightened countless souls throughout the world and from whom we ourselves have received God's grace. So now there can be no question that you will come with me to him so that he can show you how you have been fooled by the Evil One."

With this, Brother Ruffino arose and went to Saint Francis who, seeing him approach at a distance, began to shout, "Oh Brother Ruffino, foolish, foolish man! Who have you been listening to?" Saint Francis disclosed to him every temptation the Devil had used to attack him, both within and without, demonstrating to him clearly that it had been the Evil One, and not Christ, who had appeared in the vision and that he should not, for any reason whatsoever, follow any suggestions given to him by the Devil. "Indeed, should the Devil say to you, 'You are among the damned,' you should reply by saying, 'Open your mouth once more and I will shit in it.' So let this be the sign whereby you know that it is the Devil and not Christ, for if you say this to the Devil, he will surely flee. And further, you can recognize the work of the Evil One, for his task is to harden your heart to every thing that is good and worthwhile, whereas our blessed Christ never hardens the heart of a faithful man but renders it gentle and responsive at all times, as in the words of the prophet, 'I will take from you your stony heart and put within you a living heart of flesh and blood.'"

Upon hearing Saint Francis tell him word for word every temptation that he had undergone, Brother Ruffino regretted all that he had said and done and began to weep loudly, clinging to Saint Francis in love, humbly confessing his fault in having hidden these temptations from him, and after being admonished by his spiritual father, he felt greatly comforted and knew that all had changed now for the better.

In the end, Saint Francis told him, "Go, now, my son, make a full confession and do not neglect your daily prayers. This temptation you have undergone will yet be of great usefulness and consolation to you, as you will shortly find out."

Brother Ruffino returned to his cell in the woods, and after a long time weeping in prayer, the Evil One came to him once again with the outward appearance of the person of Jesus Christ, and said to him, "Oh Brother Ruffino, did I not tell you not to believe that son of Pietro Bernardoni and not to tire yourself out with so much prayer and crying, since you are among the damned? Why afflict yourself in this life with such things, since, after your death, you will be going to hell anyway?"

This time, Brother Ruffino responded quickly, "Open your mouth one more time and I will shit in it."

Having been so insulted, the Evil One instantly left that place with such an uproar and commotion that the very rocks of Mount Subasio were shaken to their base, slamming into each other as they fell and creating sparks that started a fire in the valley. Hearing the awful sound that they made, Saint Francis and his companion came out of their community house to witness what had happened and could see the great pile of boulders that lay on the ground. Thus, Brother Ruffino realized with certainty that it had been the Evil One tempting him and trying to deceive him. Going to Saint Francis once more, he threw himself at his feet and confessed his sin, whereupon Saint Francis comforted him with tender words and sent him back to his cell much consoled.

Praying here once more with deep devotion, Brother Ruffino witnessed the appearance of the blessed Christ himself. He could feel his entire soul warmed by divine love, and he heard Christ say to him, "You have done well, my son, by believing what Brother Francis has told you. It was my enemy who created that sadness in you. But I am Christ, your one true teacher and master, and so that you know it is I who come to you, I give you this sign: for the rest of your life, never again shall you feel sadness or despair." And with these words, Christ departed, leaving Brother Ruffino with such feelings of joy, sweetness of spirit, and elevation of mind that he was enraptured day and night by the glory of God.

From that point forward, he was a changed man, confirmed in grace, his spiritual health assured, and he would have spent every one of his day and nights at constant prayer and contemplation if he had been allowed to do so. Of him, Saint Francis was fond of saying that Christ had canonized him a saint in this life and would not hesitate to call him Saint Ruffino—except, of course, to his face.

Praise be to Jesus Christ and his poor servant Saint Francis. Amen.

twenty-three

The beautiful sermon Saint Francis and Brother
Ruffino preached in the nude. ⤚

Continuing Ruffino's education in how to combat spiritual pride,
Francis appears here with similar earthy directness about the
necessity of detachment from self. For those who like their saints
inoffensive, saccharine, and bloodless, this story, along with the
previous one, stands as a direct challenge to such false, affected
piety. In addition, the assertion here that their nudity is a licit form
of preaching by deed and not simply by word, presents in one more
striking way the kind of creation-affirming, body-conscious
spirituality that pervaded Francis's understanding of Christ and
the Gospel.

✢ ✢ ✢

Due to his life of continual contemplative prayer, Brother
Ruffino spoke very little, nearly senseless and dumb from
his state of constant rapture with the glory of God, such that
he had not been given the grace, nor the desire, nor the inspiration for preaching. Nevertheless, Saint Francis instructed
him one day that he was to go into the town of Assisi and
preach whatever God inspired him to preach to the people
there.

Brother Ruffino replied, "Reverend Father, I ask you most humbly to excuse me from this and not send me. As you know, I have not been endowed with the grace of preaching, for I am simple and uneducated."

Saint Francis said to him, "Because you have not promptly obeyed my instructions to you, I now command you, under holy obedience, to take off all your clothes and to go, as naked as the day you were born, wearing nothing but your underwear, into a church in Assisi and to preach to the people."

Upon this command, Brother Ruffino removed his habit and went to Assisi, where he entered a church, bowed to the altar, and climbed into the pulpit to preach. Seeing this sight, the children and townspeople began to laugh, saying, "These brothers are losing their minds with all their fasting and penance!"

Meanwhile, after thinking about the prompt obedience with which Brother Ruffino, among the noblest men in Assisi, had obeyed his harsh command, he began to regret what he had done, saying to himself, "How presumptuous of you, son of Pietro Bernardoni, wicked little man that you are, to command Brother Ruffino, one of the noblest men in Assisi, to go about preaching naked, as if he were insane! By God, you shall experience yourself what it is that you have commanded others to undergo."

So, feeling a great fervor of spirit, he undressed in a similar manner and went to Assisi, taking Brother Leo with him to carry his habit and the habit Brother Ruffino had left behind. And when the townspeople of Assisi saw him likewise going about without clothes, they mocked him and concluded that the two of them had driven themselves mad with penitence.

Saint Francis entered the church where Brother Ruffino

was preaching and heard him say, "Beloved, renounce the world and all its sin. Give everything you have to your neighbor, if you wish to avoid damnation. Honor God's commandments, love both God and your neighbor, if you wish to go to heaven. Live a life of penance, if you wish to gain the kingdom of heaven."

At this point, Saint Francis mounted the pulpit, naked as well, and began to preach so wonderfully about renunciation of earthly things, holy penitence, a life of voluntary poverty, the desire for the kingdom of heaven, and the nakedness and shame that our Lord Jesus Christ experienced in his Passion, that all who heard the sermon, both men and women, in great numbers, began to weep with devotion and compunction. Not just those in the church but the entire town of Assisi began to weep over the Passion of Christ in a way that had never been seen before or since.

So enlightened and consoled were the townspeople by these words of Saint Francis and Brother Ruffino that Saint Francis dressed himself and Brother Ruffino in their habits once again and, now clothed, went to the community house of the Porziuncola, praising and glorifying God for having granted them, through self-denial, the grace of inner strength and for being able to lead Christ's little lambs into the truth by their own example of disdain for things of this world. The devotion of the townspeople toward them grew so much from that day forward that any one who touched the hem of their habits was considered blessed.

Praise be to Jesus Christ and his poor servant Saint Francis. Amen.

twenty-four

How Saint Clare, as commanded by the Pope, blessed the bread before her on the table, and how the sign of the Cross appeared on every loaf. ⊰⊱

The same basic point as was made earlier in Francis's sermon to the birds is made here with regard to women: the Gospel demands inclusiveness. The hierarchical structures of the Church, necessary as they might be, ought to do as the Pope does here symbolically: to seek sustenance through the blessing action of all *who follow the Cross—laypeople, women, and men.*

⋆⋆⋆

SAINT CLARE, most devoted follower of the Cross of Christ and beloved spiritual daughter of Saint Francis, was of a holiness such that not only bishops and cardinals but even the Pope himself wished to visit and speak with her personally. During one such visit, when the holy father had come to her convent to hear her discourse on heavenly matters and engage her in conversation on various subjects, Saint Clare instructed that the table be set for dinner and the bread placed upon it, so that the holy father might bless it. Having concluded her spiritual discourse, Saint Clare knelt before him with great reverence and asked him if he would bless the bread on the table before them.

The holy father answered her, saying, "My faithful Sister Clare, I wish for you to bless this bread and make the sign of the Cross upon it, in that you have given yourself to that Cross so completely."

Saint Clare said to him, "Most holy Father, forgive me, but I would be worthy of severe reprimand, should I, a mere woman before the Vicar of Christ himself, dare to give such a blessing."

The Pope responded, "So that no one can accuse you of presumption but rather of complete obedience, I therefore instruct you under holy obedience to make the sign of the Cross over this bread and to bless it in the name of God."

So, being the true and obedient spiritual daughter that she was, Saint Clare blessed the bread on the table before her with the sign of the Cross. Wonder of wonders! On every loaf of bread there miraculously appeared a beautifully inscribed sign of the Cross. Some of this bread was eaten and some was saved because of this miraculous sign. The holy father, who had witnessed the miracle, took some of this bread with him when he left, thanking God and blessing Saint Clare.

At that time, there lived in the convent with Saint Clare Sister Ortolana, her mother, and Sister Agnes, her sister, who, like Saint Clare, were filled with virtue and the Holy Spirit, as were likewise many of the other saintly nuns. Saint Francis often sent those who were ailing to them, and with their prayers and the sign of the Cross, the sisters brought everyone back to full health.

Praise be to Jesus Christ and his poor servant Saint Francis. Amen.

twenty-five

How Saint Clare, while ailing, was miraculously brought to the church of Saint Francis on Christmas Eve, where she prayed the Office. ⋆⋆

Given Francis's status as friar, not ordained priest, that such explicit Eucharistic imagery appears here in conjunction with Clare makes clear the radical, if not frankly subversive, character of the spirituality of the early Franciscan movement within the medieval Church. This story brings forward certain feminine qualities to this central action in the life of the Church that remain underemphasized even today: nourishment, reception, and a mystical relationship to Christ that follows a trajectory of love, marriage, conception, and birth. At the risk of trivializing the important spiritual themes herein, we would be remiss not to acknowledge that this particular tale forms the basis for Clare having been declared the patron saint of television within the Roman Catholic Church.

⋆⋆⋆

Once, during a severe illness, Saint Clare was unable to pray the office in the chapel with the rest of the nuns. In observance of the Eve of the Solemnity of the Nativity of Christ, the nuns went to Matins as Saint Clare remained in bed, unhappy that she was unable to join them for this spiritual consolation. But Jesus Christ, her spouse, not wishing to see her suffer disconsolate, transported her miraculously to the church of Saint Francis, where she participated in Matins and at midnight Mass, and received communion, after which she was brought back to her own bed by the Lord.

As the nuns returned to her, after having prayed the Office at the church of San Damiano, they said, "Oh Sister Clare, holy mother, what great consolation we have received during this time of Nativity! Had it pleased God, we would have wished that you had been there with us."

To this Saint Clare answered, "Praise and thanks be to our blessed Lord Jesus Christ, dear sisters and beloved daughters of mine, for I have observed all the offices of this most holy of nights, along with some you yourselves did not observe, and find my soul much consoled for it. Saint Francis, my father, interceded for me and by the grace of our Lord Jesus Christ, I was able to see and hear with my own ears the entire office, indeed even the sound of the organ being played, and received Holy Communion as well. So for this grace given to me, rejoice and give thanks to God."

Praise be to Jesus Christ and his poor servant Saint Francis. Amen.

twenty-six

How Saint Francis explained to Brother Leo the
meaning of a vision he had seen. ⤙

*This story is one of the last in the collection in which Francis appears
directly. The profound and multilayered image of the river, shared by
so many religious traditions, is, we think, a fitting end to the stories
that focus upon the heart of Francis's own spiritual teaching.*

✻ ✻ ✻

DURING A TIME when Saint Francis was gravely ill and
Brother Leo was tending to him, Brother Leo prayed beside
him and became enraptured. In his state of ecstasy, he felt
himself taken in spirit to the banks of an enormous river,
wide and full of rapids, and standing there to watch who
would pass, he saw several brothers enter into the river,
heavily laden, only to see them quickly taken by the current
and drowned. Some made it about a third of the way into the
river, some halfway, some nearly all the way across, but all
of them, due to the strong current and the heavy loads they
were carrying, ultimately lost their footing and went under.
In witnessing this, Brother Leo felt within himself a great
compassion for them, but then, still standing there, he saw a
great multitude of others friars approaching, carrying noth-

ing whatsoever on their backs, a sign of their dedication to holy poverty. Thus, they entered the same river and crossed over without any problem whatsoever, at which point, Brother Leo came back to himself.

Saint Francis, feeling within his spirit that Brother Leo had been given a vision, called to him and asked him what he had seen, and having been instructed thus, Brother Leo recounted the entire vision to Saint Francis, who then said, "What you have seen is the truth. The great river is this world, and the friars who drowned in the river are those who do not remain faithful to their Gospel profession, in particular, their vow of poverty. Those, however, that have no problem crossing over are those friars who do not cling to things of the flesh and who possess no earthly belongings but who, on the contrary, live temperately and dress modestly. They are happy to follow Christ naked to his cross and bear the weight of his yoke, that is to say, holy obedience, joyfully and willingly, and thus they pass from this earthly life into life eternal with ease."

Praise be to Jesus Christ and his poor servant Saint Francis. Amen.

Reflections on the Stigmata ⤙⤚

Saint Francis was the first person in the Western Christian tradition to have received the stigmata, the wounds of Christ, and this carefully composed and exceedingly dramatic account of Francis's manifestation of this particular sign of grace is at the same time an account of his death. Once having read the five acts of these "reflections," it makes sense that Francis, who lived out his life in increasing, mystical union with the Crucified One, would in the end became absorbed fully, literally, into that experience of divine selflessness.

Though the central section of the story receives the most attention, the latter part of the account has some very interesting features. For example, Francis is consistently presented as being quite secretive about the wounds and the mystical revelations he received, reminding one of Jesus's own wariness of revealing himself as the Messiah in the Gospel accounts, and also reflecting the pattern often seen in subsequent hagiographic or apparition accounts of "secrets" told to mystics, not to be revealed in this life. The utter originality of God's action in this imposition of the stigmata is what renders their verification so much a concern for those around Francis and for the writer of this account.

Apart from these features of the narrative itself, the account has the effect of raising more questions than it answers. What do the stigmata mean, and what is God's purpose behind these unusual signs—for Francis receiving them, for the people around him who witnessed them, and for us so many centuries later reading about them? What do they teach us? How do they speak to us—about suffering, about selflessness, about the contemplative life, about affective union with God, about the role of our bodies in the life of our soul? Like the crucifixion itself, these wounds are the shocking, graphic, and altogether consistent result of the unique Christian revelation in Jesus: that the Creator God so loved the world as to take on, willingly, an incarnate form, an ordinary body subject to death in the course of time and history, so as to show how all of us might, ultimately, find our way back to a full share in the life of divinity.

⁕ ⁕ ⁕

HERE WILL BE PRESENTED an account of the sacred, glorious, and most holy stigmata received by our holy father Saint Francis, given to him by Christ on holy Mount Alverno. Because this image of the wounds of our Lord Jesus Christ numbered five, there will be five parts to our account: First, how Saint Francis came to holy Mount Alverno. Second, how he lived there and his conversations with those whom he took with him to the holy mountain. Third, the appearance of the seraph and the imposition of the Sacred Stigmata. Fourth, how Saint Francis descended from Mount Alverno once he had received the Sacred Stigmata and returned to Santa Maria degli Angeli. Fifth, certain apparitions and divine revelations that occurred after the death of Saint Francis to certain saintly friars and other devout persons concerning the glorious Sacred Stigmata.

I

Saint Francis, at the age of forty-three, in the year 1224, was inspired by God to leave the valley of Spoleto and journey to Romagna with Brother Leo as his companion. Traveling on foot, they passed by the Castle of Montefeltro, where a great banquet with many solemn festivities were being held to honor one of the counts of Montefeltro, who was to be knighted. Hearing of these celebrations and that many noblemen would be in attendance from a number of different countries, Saint Francis said to Brother Leo, "Come, let us go up to this banquet, so that, with God's help, we may gather from it much spiritual fruit."

Among the many highborn men who had come to this banquet was a very well-known, rich nobleman from Tuscany, one Signor Orlando da Chiusi di Casentino, who had heard of the many miracles and great holiness of Saint Francis and thus felt a great devotion toward him and fervently wished to see him and hear him preach. Upon reaching the courtyard of the castle, Saint Francis entered into the large crowd of those assembled for the banquet and, seized with spiritual fervor, climbed up onto a low wall and began to preach in the vernacular language, using as his text the common saying, "So great is the good that I expect to receive that all pain is as joy to me." Inspired by the Holy Spirit, he preached devoutly and with deep insight upon this theme, using as examples the various trials endured by the apostles, the willing deaths suffered by the martyrs, the austere penances undertaken by the confessors, and the many tribulations and temptations overcome by virgins and other saints, such that the eyes of everyone in the courtyard were fixed upon him, attending to his every word as if an angel of God were speaking to them.

Among them, Signor Orlando felt God touch his heart through this wonderful sermon by Saint Francis and was resolved by the end of it to put his life and his soul in proper order. Thus, afterward, he went to Saint Francis, took him aside, and said to him, "Holy Father, I would like your assistance in putting my soul aright."

Saint Francis replied, "It gives me great joy to hear this, but for now, please join the festivities to which you have been invited by your friends, and after the banquet, we shall speak with one another again."

So Signor Orlando attended the banquet and afterward, as Saint Francis had said, they conversed together at great length concerning what he needed to do for the sake of his soul's salvation. At the end of their talk together, Signor Orlando said to Saint Francis, "I have a mountain in Tuscany called Mount Alverno, a very holy and solitary place, at a great remove from anyone or anything, and so it is especially suited to anyone who might wish to withdraw on penitential retreat or to live a life of contemplative solitude. If you see fit, I would gladly donate this mountain to you and your companions for your use, for the sake of my soul."

When Saint Francis heard him so generously offering them a place that he and his companions could most certainly use, he rejoiced, praising and thanking God, first, and then Signor Orlando: "Dear sir, when you return home, I will send one of my companions to you and you can take him to this mountain, and if he deems it suitable for a life of prayer and penance, I will then accept this most loving gift you are offering to me." And with this, Saint Francis set off again, and having completed his journey, he returned to Santa Maria degli Angeli. Likewise, after the conclusion of the festivities, Signor Orlando went back to his home, the castle of Chiusi, which was about a mile distant from Mount Alverno.

Once at Santa Maria degli Angeli, Saint Francis sent two of his companions to Signor Orlando and they were received by him with great generosity and happiness. Wishing to show them Mount Alverno, he sent them off with a guard of fifty armed men to protect them from the wild animals, and so accompanied, the two friars went up to explore the mountain and found a place on it that was indeed quite well suited for a life of contemplation. They chose a level meadow as the location where they, along with Saint Francis, could live. With the help of the men guarding them, they made some little cells for themselves using tree branches, and in this way, accepted and took possession of Mount Alverno, establishing a community there, after which they departed and returned to Saint Francis, to whom they recounted all the events that had transpired on Mount Alverno which was, they said, truly well suited for prayer and contemplation.

Upon hearing their report, Saint Francis was exceedingly happy, praising and thanking the Lord, his face beaming as he said to the friars, "Beloved sons, the Lent of Saint Michael is drawing close and I firmly believe that it is God's will for us to spend these forty days on Mount Alverno, which, through divine providence, has been prepared for us to render glory and honor to the Lord, to the Blessed Virgin Mary, and to all the holy angels, such that through penitence and prayer, we might be worthy of the consolation afforded to us through the consecration of this blessed mountain."

With these words, then, Saint Francis gathered to him Brother Masseo da Marignano from Assisi, a man of great intellect and eloquence, and Brother Angelo Tancredi from Rieti, a nobleman who had served as a knight before entering religious life, along with Brother Leo, whose purity and simplicity of soul was much beloved by Saint Francis, who confided in him all the secrets of his own heart. Along with these three friars, Saint Francis began to pray, and having finished his prayers, asked for the prayers of all the remaining friars. Then the four set off for Mount Alverno, in the name of the Crucified Christ.

On the way, Saint Francis called to Brother Masseo and said, "You, Brother Masseo, shall be our guardian and superior on this journey. While we are traveling together or taking our rest, we will thus observe our usual customs: maintaining silence except when praying the Office or speaking of the Lord; giving no thought beforehand of what we shall eat or drink or where we shall lay our heads; begging daily for our bread; and taking our rest in whatever place God sees fit to provide us." His companions nodded their heads in agreement and, making the sign of the cross, went upon their way together.

That first evening, they reached a community house and stayed with the friars there. The second evening, due to inclement weather and their own fatigue, they were unable to make their way to either a community house or any nearby town, and so took refuge that stormy night in an abandoned, dilapidated church, where they at last lay their heads down to sleep.

While his companions were asleep, Saint Francis rose to pray, and during this first part of the night, a great multitude of fierce demons came upon him, roaring in a great frenzy and attacking him from all around, this way and that, in order to disturb his prayer, pushing him from behind and from in front, pulling him up and down, shouting at him, threatening him, reproaching him. In the end, however, they were unable to disturb him, for God was with him, until finally, having sustained this assault for quite some time, he raised his voice over the battle and said, "Accursed spirits, you can do nothing unless God himself permits you to do it. So, in the name of God Almighty, I tell you that whatever you do to my body, God himself is permitting you to do, which is why I gladly endure whatever comes to me, for I have no greater enemy than my body. Thus, if you seek to take your revenge upon my body, know that you are doing my soul a very great favor."

Upon hearing this, the demons grew even more furious and began to drag him all about the empty church, seeking to injure him even more seriously than before, but after it all Saint Francis simply shouted more loudly still, "My Lord Jesus Christ, I thank you for the generosity and love you are showing me here, which is a sign of your infinite charity, for when the Lord punishes his servant thoroughly in this life, he does so to avoid having to punish him in the next. For this reason I am prepared to joyfully endure any affliction or adversity you wish to send me on account of my sins."

At long last, the demons, confused by his patience and firmness of heart, took their leave from him, and Saint Francis, with a fervor of spirit, left the church and went into the woods close by, where he began to pray, weeping and beating his chest, longing for his lover Jesus Christ, his soul's delight, who came to him in the depths of his heart that night. Saint Francis spoke to Christ as if to his master and received his replies as if from a judge, at times pleading with him as if with a father, but also conversing with him as if with an intimate friend. Throughout that night, his companions could hear him from the woods and watched over him from a distance as he prayed devoutly for God's mercy on sinners, crying out in pain over the Passion of Christ as if he were seeing it himself, with his very own eyes. That night the friars beheld him with his arms outstretched, as if on a cross, raised up into the air above the ground, surrounded by a wondrous light, and so he stayed for quite some time, spending the entire night in such devotion and never sleeping.

The next morning, knowing that Saint Francis had not slept the previous night and thus would be too weak to continue his journey on foot, his companions went off and asked one of the peasants in the area if he would, for the love of God, lend them his donkey for the use of Saint Francis, who could no longer continue on foot.

Upon hearing the name of Saint Francis, the man said, "Are you brothers of that Brother Francis about whom we hear so many wonderful things?"

They replied that, yes, they were, and that they were asking on his behalf for the donkey. Upon hearing this, the workman saddled his donkey with great solicitude and devotion and took it himself to Saint Francis, who climbed upon it with deepest gratitude. They all then continued on their way, Saint Francis following behind them on the donkey.

After traveling a short stretch, the peasant said to Saint Francis, "Tell me, are you really Brother Francis of Assisi?"

Saint Francis said that, yes, he was.

"Well, then, I am warning you," said the man, "you better be as holy a man as everyone says you are, because a lot of people have faith in you, and I'm telling you now, you better live up to your reputation and not disappoint everyone."

Having heard these words, Saint Francis did not take offense, and didn't say to himself, "Who is this creature admonishing me?" as many a proud friar in a habit these days might well say in response. Rather, Saint Francis threw himself down off the donkey, knelt before the peasant, and kissed his feet, thanking him in all humility for having been so charitable as to admonish him, after which the local man and Saint Francis's companions picked him up off the ground, placed him back on the donkey, and continued on their way.

Halfway up the road toward the mountain, because it was very hot and the climb upward was difficult, the peasant began to cry out in great thirst, "This is killing me. If I don't get something to drink, I'm going to pass out."

Hearing this, Saint Francis got off the donkey and knelt down in prayer, and with his hands raised to heaven, he knew that God had heard his prayer. "Go," he said to the peasant, "go quick to that rock and there you will find a spring of living water that Christ himself, in his mercy, has provided us."

The peasant ran over to the rock that Saint Francis had pointed toward and there, indeed, was a beautiful spring flowing forth from the hard rock, by virtue of Saint Francis's prayers, and he drank deeply of the water and was entirely refreshed. That this spring was produced by Saint Francis's prayers that day is certain, for neither before nor since has anyone seen a spring of water in that place. Saint Francis and his companions, along with the peasant, gave thanks to God for this miracle and continued on their way.

As they drew near to the mountain, Saint Francis dismounted and rested on the side of the road beneath a large oak tree, which can still be seen in that place. While he was there, looking out upon the mountain and the surrounding country, considering the lay of the land, a great flock of various birds began to fly about, singing and beating their wings happily as if in festive celebration, and they crowded about Saint Francis, some landing on his head, some on his shoulders, some on his arms and chest, some at his feet. When his companions and the peasants beheld this wonderful sight, Saint Francis, rejoicing in spirit, said to them, "I do believe, beloved brothers, that our Lord Jesus Christ wishes us to reside here on this solitary mountain, since we are being welcomed with such happiness by these little brothers and sisters of ours, the birds." And they continued onward until they finally came to the place that the earlier friars had chosen for their habitation.

This, then, is the first part of the story, how Saint Francis first came to Mount Alverno.

Praise be to our Lord Jesus Christ and his poor servant Francis. Amen.

II

The second part concerns conversations Saint Francis had with his companions on the mountain.

When Signor Orlando received word that Saint Francis and his three companions had gone up to live on Mount Alverno, he was filled with joy, and the following day went out with many others from his castle to visit Saint Francis, bringing bread, wine, and other necessities of life for him and his companions. Upon reaching the place, he found them in prayer and drawing near, he greeted them, whereupon Saint Francis arose and received Signor Orlando and his company with great warmth and happiness.

As they began to converse, Saint Francis thanked him for this holy mountain that he had given them and for his visit, and Saint Francis asked Orlando if he might have made for him a small cell at the foot of a beautiful beech tree, about a stone's throw from the place where the other friars would be living, since that place seemed quite suitable for devotion and contemplation. Orlando immediately saw to it that the cell be built.

Evening was drawing close and so, too, the time for Orlando and his company's departure, but before they left, Saint Francis preached to them a while, and after hearing his preaching and receiving his blessing, Signor Orlando took Saint Francis and his companions aside before leaving and said, "Beloved friars, I have no intention of leaving you here on this deserted mountain without providing for your corporal needs, without which you can hardly attend to spiritual matters. So, I enjoin you to send to my house for whatever you need, and should you not do so, I will be greatly troubled." And in saying this, he left with his company and returned to the castle.

Saint Francis called his companions together and began to instruct them on the way of life they—and whoever else was called by the Lord—were to live in this wilderness. Among many things, he emphasized in a special way their holy observance of poverty. "Pay no attention to the generous offer made to us by our Lord Orlando, lest you offend our true mistress, our beloved Lady Poverty. You may be sure that, if we show her disdain, the world will show us that much more disdain and we shall find ourselves in even greater need of her, but if we cling close to Lady Poverty, the world shall see to it that we are supplied abundantly with all that we require. The Lord has called us into religious life for the salvation of the world, and this is the covenant between the world and ourselves, that we provide a good example to the world so that it may provide us with what we require. Let us then hold fast to Blessed Poverty, since she shows us the way to perfection and holds the promise and pledge of our true spiritual wealth."

After speaking quite devoutly for some time on this and other matters, Saint Francis concluded his discourse, saying, "This is the way of life that you and I shall live, and though I find myself at the point of death, I intend henceforth to live in solitude, to bring myself fully to the Lord, and to repent of my sinfulness before him. When he feels it is time, Brother Leo will bring me some bread and a bit of water, and I will receive no visitors. Whatever any visitor desires, please see to them on my behalf." And having said these words, he blessed them and withdrew into his cell beneath the beech tree, and his companions returned to their community house, firmly resolved to follow all his instructions to them.

A few days after, as Saint Francis stood next to his cell, meditating upon the landscape of the mountain and marveling at the enormous canyons and fissures that he could see there between all the enormous rocks, he began to pray. It pleased God to reveal to him that these enormous canyons had been made at the hour of Christ's Passion when, as the Evangelist has written, the earth shook and the rocks were split. It was God's will that this happen upon Mount Alverno so that in that place, the Passion of our Lord Jesus Christ might be renewed in love and compassion in the soul and the body of his humble servant through the sign of the most holy Sacred Stigmata.

With this revelation, Saint Francis withdrew into his cell and gathered his spirit, opening himself to the mystery of this revelation, and from that time forward, Saint Francis engaged in continual prayer, drinking in ever more deeply the sweetness of divine contemplation, often so enraptured with God that his companions often saw him suspended, ecstatic, in midair.

During these states of contemplative ecstasy, God revealed to him not only present and future things, but also the secret thoughts and desires of the friars, as Brother Leo himself found out one day. Having battled for some time a very powerful temptation, of the spirit, though, not of the flesh, Brother Leo greatly desired to have from the hand of Saint Francis some holy words of encouragement, thinking that such a token would either lessen or completely banish this temptation altogether. Entertaining this wish, however, out of shame and reverence, he did not dare speak it to Saint Francis.

Yet, what he had not told Saint Francis, the Holy Spirit did, and so Saint Francis called to Brother Leo and asked him to bring him pen and paper, upon which he wrote some lines in praise of Christ, as the friar had wished for, and signing it with a single Tau, he gave it to him, saying, "Beloved Brother, take this paper and guard it diligently for the rest of your life. May the Lord bless you and keep from all temptation. Do not be troubled or afraid if you feel tempted, for I know you are a friend and faithful servant of God, and the more beloved you become, the more you shall be assailed by temptation. Truly I say to you that no one becomes perfect in love for the Lord without passing through many trials and temptations."

Taking this note with profound devotion and faith, Brother Leo quickly felt all temptation leave him, and upon his return to the community house, with great joy he recounted to his companions the grace that the Lord had granted him in this note from the hand of Saint Francis, and by keeping it close and consulting it often, the friars accomplished many miracles through it.

From that time forward, Brother Leo, with great purity of heart and resolution of will, began to pay close attention to the way Saint Francis was living, and because of this purity and resolution, he was granted occasion more and more often to see the saint rapt in ecstasy, suspended in air, sometimes as high as three or four yards above the ground, several times as high as the top of the beech tree, sometimes so high in the air and surrounded with such a brilliance that he could hardly bear to look at him.

And what did this simple friar do when Saint Francis was suspended just high enough above the earth that he could reach him? At those times, he went to him softly and embraced his feet, kissing them and weeping, "My Lord, have mercy on me, a sinner, and by the merits of this holy man, help me find my way to your grace." Once, when Saint Francis had been lifted from the earth in ecstasy higher than Brother Leo could reach, he stood beneath his feet, and a scroll descended from heaven and came to rest on Saint Francis's head. Upon the scroll were letters of gold reading, "Here is God's grace." After Brother Leo read this saying, he saw the scroll return to heaven whence it came.

Endowed by God's grace, Saint Francis not only was enraptured in contemplative ecstasy but also was comforted, several times, by angelic visitations. One day, thinking of his own death and of what would happen to the Order afterward, he said, "Lord God, what shall become of your poor little family after I have died, this little family that you in your kindness have entrusted to me? Who will comfort them? Who will correct them? Who will pray for them?"

While he was saying these and other similar words, an angel sent by God appeared to him and reassured him, saying, "On behalf of God, I tell you that the Order you have founded will last until the day of judgment and that there is no sinner so wicked who, out of love for the Order, cannot help but find God's mercy. And no one who out of malice persecutes the Order shall live long. And further, any wicked person in the Order who does not correct his ways will not remain in the Order for long, so do not grow sad when you see friars in the Order who are lazy and who do not observe the Rule as they ought. Do not think that the Order shall be harmed on their account, for there will be many, many friars who will follow the Gospel way of life given by Christ and will perfect themselves in the purity of the Rule. These will pass from this life quickly into life eternal without passing through a time of purification, for God will forgo their purgatory. Do not worry about all those who do not observe the Rule, says the Lord, for they are his concern." And having said these words, the angel left and Saint Francis felt greatly comforted and consoled.

As the Feast of the Assumption of Our Lady grew close, Saint Francis began to seek out an even more solitary place where he might spend the time of the Lent of Saint Michael the Archangel, which begins on the Feast of the Assumption. Thus, he called to Brother Leo and said to him, "Stand in the doorway of the chapel of the community house, and when you hear me call, turn my way."

So Brother Leo went and stood in the doorway, and Saint Francis walked away some distance and then called out loudly. Hearing him, Brother Leo turned toward him, and Saint Francis said to him, "My son, let's see if we can find an even more solitary place, where you cannot hear me when I call to you."

After seeking for a time, they came upon a spot on the side of the northerly face of the mountain that was well suited for his purposes, very solitary, but he could not make his way there, for in between there lay an enormous rocky chasm, steep and fearful. So with great effort they placed a large piece of wood over the chasm to serve as a kind of bridge, and using it, they were able to reach the place.

Saint Francis then sent for the other friars, told them that it was his intention to spend the Lent of Saint Michael in this place of solitude and asked them to build him a small cell, here where no one could hear him shouting. They did as he asked, and once the cell was built, he said to them, "You may now return to the house and leave me here by myself. With the help of God, my intention is to spend these forty days without anything to disturb my peace of mind and without visitors of any kind, religious or laypeople. Only you, Brother Leo, by yourself, may bring me bread and water once during the day and again at night, at the hour of Matins, coming here in silence and upon reaching the bridge, saying simply, "Lord, open my lips." If at that time I answer you, cross over and come into my cell where we will pray the Office together. If I do not answer you, you are to leave right away." Saint Francis gave these instructions, for when he was rapt in ecstasy, he heard nothing nor was he able to feel anything in his body. In conclusion, Saint Francis blessed the friars and they returned to their house.

Upon the Feast of the Assumption, Saint Francis began his holy Lent, observing great abstinence and austerity, disciplining his body in a way that was comforting to his soul, engaging in fervent prayers, vigils, and ascetic practices, whereby he grew continually in virtue, disposing his soul to receive divine mysteries and heavenly splendor.

His body endured many cruel battles with demonic powers that often assailed him through his senses. At one time during this Lent, having left his cell with a fervent spirit to go pray near a grave that had been carved from a rock high on the side of the mountain above a horrible and fearsome precipice, the Evil One came to him in a storm of noise of disturbance. Frightening in his appearance, the Evil One battered Saint Francis about in attempt to push him over the edge. Having no place to escape to and being quite unable to stand up against the cruelty of the Devil, he turned and placed his hands firmly on the rock, turned his face toward God, and placed himself under his protection, holding on so tightly with his hands that nothing could drag him away. As it is always God's will to refrain from tempting his servants more than they are able to bear, suddenly the rock collapsed inward, miraculously conforming itself to the very shape of Saint Francis's body, holding him safely there, as if he had placed his hands and face into melted wax that was now imprinted with the shape of his hands and face. In this way, with God's help, he was able to escape the power of the Devil.

Though the Evil One was unable to accomplish his intention and did not succeed in pushing Saint Francis over the edge of the precipice, such a fate he did manage to wreak, much later, after the death of Saint Francis, upon one of his beloved and devoted friars. This friar found himself one day in the same place, preparing some pieces of wood to assure the safety of those who might come there out of devotion to Saint Francis and in honor of the miracle that had taken place. While the friar was carrying a piece of heavy wood on his shoulder, the Evil One tripped him, and over the edge he fell with the wood he was carrying on top of him.

But God, who had rescued and preserved Saint Francis from falling, by Saint Francis's merits likewise rescued and preserved his devoted brother from the danger of his fall. Crying aloud as he fell for Saint Francis to keep him safe, the friar saw Saint Francis suddenly appear and bear him up, placing him on a rock without a single bruise or wound. Having heard the cry of the brother as he fell and certain that he had been crushed and killed on the sharp rocks below, the other friars prepared a casket and went around to the other side of mountain in order to recover the pieces of his body and bury them. There they came upon the brother who had fallen, on his feet, still carrying the large plank of wood, singing the Te Deum in a loud voice.

Completely amazed, they heard him recount everything that had occurred during his fall and how Saint Francis had rescued him from danger, so they all returned home and together sang the Te Deum, praising and thanking the Lord and Saint Francis for the miracle that had been granted their brother.

Throughout the Lent, as it has already been said, he sustained many assaults by the Evil One but also received much consolation from the Lord, not only in the form of angelic visitations but also by way of the wild birds. During these forty days, a falcon made its nest near his cell and every night, just before the hour of Matins, it awakened him by singing and flapping its wings, and it did not stop until he had gotten up and prayed the Office, though when from time to time Saint Francis was more tired than usual, or weak or ill, just like a wise and compassionate friend, the bird would wait until later to begin its song. Saint Francis took great delight in this holy little creature, for its solicitude on his behalf. In the night, it inspired him to pray in spite of his fatigue, and by day, it often dwelt with him as would a companion.

To conclude the second part of the story, his continued asceticism and the many battles he sustained with the Evil One left Saint Francis in a much weakened state, and seeking to nourish his body on the spiritual food of his soul's progress, he began to contemplate the endless glory and joy of the blessed ones who had passed into life eternal, and he prayed to God that he might grant him the grace of tasting just a small part of this joy.

While praying thus, suddenly an angel in great splendor appeared to him, holding in its left hand a viola and in its right a bow. Stunned by the appearance of this angel, Saint Francis saw it draw the bow across the viola and at once, such a sweet melody pervaded Saint Francis's soul and lifted it above any bodily feeling that, according to what he recounted to his companions later, he feared that, had the angel drawn the bow a second time, the intolerable sweetness of the sound would have taken his soul from his body altogether.

This is the end of the second part.

Praise be to Jesus Christ and to his poor servant Saint Francis. Amen.

III

This third part will recount the apparition of the seraph and the imposition of the Sacred Stigmata, while the feast of the Holy Cross was drawing near in the month of September.

One night, at the usual hour, Brother Leo went to the place where Saint Francis would usually recite Matins, and at the foot of the walkway, as he usually did, he said, "Lord, open my lips." That night, Saint Francis said nothing in reply, but instead of returning to his house as Saint Francis had instructed him, with every good and holy intention Brother Leo crossed over the bridge and went into Saint Francis's cell. Not finding him there, Brother Leo thought that he might be in the woods praying and set out by the light of the moon to look about the woods for him, and hearing Saint Francis's voice, he drew near and saw him on his knees in prayer, face and hands lifted toward heaven, exclaiming fervently, "Oh my sweetest Lord, who are you? And who am I, your wicked and useless worm of a servant?" repeating these words over and over.

Marveling at this sight, Brother Leo raised his eyes and saw in the heavens a beautiful, flaming torch coming down, which lit upon Saint Francis's head, and from its flame he heard the sound of a voice speaking with Saint Francis, though he could not understand what it was saying. Seeing these things but feeling quite unworthy to be so close to such a holy place and such a wonderful vision, and fearing that Saint Francis would be upset with him for perhaps disturbing him, he backed away and stood at a distance, waiting for the apparition to end. Three times Saint Francis held his hands out to the flame and after a long time, the torch rose back into the heavens.

Saint Francis then arose, sure-footed, rejoicing in the vision, and returned to his cell.

On his way, though, Saint Francis heard the rustle of footsteps in the leaves and called out loudly that he should wait there and should not move. So Brother Leo obediently did so, standing still and waiting with such trepidation that, according to what he said to the other friars afterward, he would have preferred for the earth to swallow him up than to stand there and await Saint Francis, who he believed was angry with him. For fear of being sent away by him, Brother Leo did all that he could to make sure never to anger his spiritual father.

Saint Francis came to him then and said, "Who are you?"

Trembling, Brother Leo replied, "My father, I am Brother Leo."

Saint Francis then asked, "And why have you come here, my little brother lamb? Did I not tell you not to come here and watch over me? Tell me under holy obedience what it is that you have seen or heard."

Brother Leo answered, "Father, I heard you speaking and repeating the words, 'Oh my sweetest Lord, who are you? And who am I, your wicked and useless worm of a servant?'" And kneeling before him, Brother Leo confessed his transgression of obedience to Saint Francis and begged his forgiveness with much weeping. He then humbly asked Saint Francis to explain what those words meant and to tell him the words spoken in reply that he had not been able to hear.

Seeing that God had permitted this humble friar Leo, so pure and simple, to see and hear these things, Saint Francis disclosed to him what he asked. "My little brother lamb in Jesus Christ, when I was repeating those words that you heard, two lights were shining within my soul, one was vision and knowledge of myself, the other vision and knowledge of the Creator. So, when I was saying, 'Oh my sweetest Lord, who are you?' I had entered into the light of contemplation, in which I was able to see into the deep abyss of God's infinite goodness, wisdom, and power. And when I was saying, 'And who am I, your wicked and useless worm of a servant?' I had entered into the other light of contemplation, in which I was able to see the pitiable depths of my own miserable life, and was saying, 'Who are you, oh God of such infinite goodness, wisdom, and power, that you should deign to visit me, a wicked, abominable worm?'

"And the flame you witnessed was God, who in that form spoke to me as he had to Moses, and among the many things he said, he asked me for three things, to which I replied, 'My Lord, I belong completely to you. You know I have only my tunic, pants, and waist-cord, and these three things are yours. What can I possibly offer up to your majesty?'

"The Lord then said to me, 'Look at your lap and offer up to me what you find there.'

"So I looked down and saw a small golden ball and offered it up to God, doing this three times as God commanded me to do, and kneeling three times, I blessed and thanked the Lord, who had given me these offerings, and in an instant I understood that these three offerings were holy obedience, glorious poverty, and a most splendid chastity, the perfect observance of which, I knew with a clear conscience, the Lord, in his grace, had granted me. And as you saw, I put my hands into my lap three times and offered up to God the three virtues, the sign of which were the three golden balls God had placed there.

"Thus God granted virtue to my soul, and for all the blessings and graces he had granted me from his infinite kindness, with my lips and my heart I praise and thank him continuously. These are the words that you heard as I raised my hands three times. But I tell you, my little brother lamb, be careful not to go about watching me, and go back to your own cell with God's blessing. Keep me in your thoughts and prayers, for in a few days, God will do such wonderful and miraculous things upon this mountain that the entire world will be amazed, new and wonderful things that have never before been done to any creature on earth."

And with these words, Saint Francis had the book of the Gospel brought to him, for the Lord had inspired him to open the Gospel three times in order to show him what God wished him to do. With Scripture in hand, he knelt down in prayer and afterward, as Brother Leo held the book, he opened it three times in the name of the Holy Trinity, and it was God's will that three times he opened it to the Passion of Christ. So he came to understand that, just as he had followed Christ in all he had done in his own life, he would now have to follow and be conformed to the suffering Christ endured through his Passion before he passed from this life.

From that moment onward, Saint Francis began to feel himself pervaded by the sweetness of divine contemplation and divine visitations, one of which prepared him for the reception of the Sacred Stigmata in this way. On the eve of the Feast of the Holy Cross, in the month of September, as Saint Francis was praying privately in his cell, an angel of God appeared to him, sent by God to say, "I am here to reassure you and to admonish you to prepare yourself humbly and to be disposed in patience to receive that which the Lord wants to give you and to do through you."

Saint Francis replied, "I am prepared to bear patiently everything that my Lord wishes to do to me," and the angel departed.

The following day, on the Feast of the Holy Cross, Saint Francis was praying before dawn in the doorway of his cell, his face turned toward the east, saying the following words, "Oh my Lord Jesus Christ, I ask you two graces before I die: the first, that, while I live, I might feel in my body and soul, as much as is possible, the suffering that you, sweet Jesus, endured in the hour of your bitterest Passion; the second, that I might feel in my heart, as much as is possible, the boundless love that, Son of God, burned within you to so willingly accept suffering for sinners such as us." And after much time in prayer, he knew that God would grant his request and that, as far as was possible for a mortal creature, he would be granted that which he asked to share with Christ.

Being promised this, Saint Francis began to devote himself to a contemplation of Christ's Passion and his infinite love, and his devotion grew continuously until all began to be transformed into Jesus, in love and in compassion. Enflamed with such contemplation, that morning, he saw a seraph descending from heaven resplendent with six fiery wings, and as it flew quickly toward him, he could see and knew clearly, from the way it held its wings, that it bore within it the image of the Crucified One, two wings above its head, two spread to fly, two wings covering its feet.

Seeing this, Saint Francis was greatly afraid and at the same time filled with wonder, sorrow, and joy. He rejoiced in the beauty of Christ approaching him so intimately and gazing upon him with such graciousness, but on the other hand, seeing him crucified upon the cross, he felt endless grief and compassion. Before this stupendous and unusual vision, he was filled with wonder, knowing that the brokenness of crucifixion could not be reconciled with the immortality of the seraphic spirit, and in his state of wonderment, it was revealed to him by the one who appeared before him that this vision had been given him in this form by divine providence so that he might understand how it would not be bodily martyrdom but rather an all-consuming spiritual fire that would transform him completely into the image of Christ Crucified.

In this vision, all of Mount Alverno appeared ablaze with a splendid fire that shone out and lit up all the mountains and valleys around it, as if it were the sun on earth. Hence, the shepherds that were in the fields about the region were terrified, seeing the mountain in flames and brilliantly lit, as they told the brothers later, attesting to how the fire burned on Mount Alverno for longer than an hour. Likewise, the splendor of this light shone through the windows of the nearby inns, such that mule drivers from Romagna got up out of bed, thinking that the sun had risen, saddling and loading their beasts, starting out upon the road until the light of the mountain had faded and the true sun had come up.

In this seraphic apparition, Christ spoke to Saint Francis of many divine secrets that Saint Francis never revealed to anyone while he lived but that, after his death, he saw fit to disclose, as will later be told.

And the words he heard were the following: "Do you know," said Christ, "what I have done for you? I have given you the stigmata that are the signs of my Passion, so that you will be my standard-bearer. Just as I, on the day of my death, went down into the underworld and rescued the souls there by virtue of my wounds, so, too, on the day of your death, you may rescue all the souls of the three Orders, Friars Minors, Sisters, and the Penitents, and all the others who had in their lives been devoted to you, raising them up to the glory of heaven by virtue of your wounds. In your death you may be conformed to me, as you were in your life."

After a long time, this wondrous vision faded, and along with its many secret revelations, the heart of Saint Francis burned with a boundless, divine love, leaving upon his body the wondrous image and marks of the Passion of Christ. On his hands and feet there appeared the marks of the nails, just as he had seen on the body of Jesus Christ Crucified in the form of the seraph. Indeed, his hands and feet appeared to have been pieced through by nails, the head of the nails clearly visible in the palms of his hands and soles of his feet, the point of the nails likewise visible on the backs of his hands and feet, almost as if they had been twisted and bent back in such a way as to stand out from his flesh, almost as if one might put a finger through them, as if through a piercing ring, and the heads of the nails were round and black. On his side appeared the mark of a lance, the wound still open, red, and bleeding such that the blood from the holy side of Saint Francis stained his tunic and pants. Therefore, his companions, before they heard from him what had happened, began to notice that he kept his hands and feet covered at all times and that he was unable to put the soles of his feet on the ground. Finding his tunic and trousers covered in blood when they washed them, they understood that he had been marked on his hands, feet, and side with the image and likeness of our crucified Lord Jesus Christ.

Though he tried mightily to hide these glorious Sacred Stigmata, so clearly marked into his flesh, he could see how poorly he was concealing these signs from his everyday companions. Yet, afraid to disclose the secrets of God, he felt within him a great doubt as to whether or not he should reveal the seraphic vision and the impression of the Sacred Stigmata he had received. Finally, spurred by his conscience, he called several of his most trusted friars to himself and discussed his doubts concerning this matter in a general way, without saying anything specific, and he asked their advice.

Among these friars was a man of great holiness named Brother Illuminato, for he was truly enlightened in God, and understanding that Saint Francis must have seen wondrous things, said to him, "Brother Francis, you must realize that it was not only to you, but to others as well, that the Lord has revealed his mysteries. You are right to be afraid that, if you withhold that which God wishes to disclose for the good of others, you might be worthy of reproach."

Moved by these words, Saint Francis then told them, with much trepidation, about the form and manner of the vision, adding, however, that Christ in his appearance to him had told him certain things that he would never reveal during his lifetime.

Though these holy wounds, because they had been given him by Christ, inspired in his heart a great joy, nevertheless they were a source of unbearable pain to his body, and constrained by this, he disclosed everything to Brother Leo, the simplest and most pure-hearted among them all. Saint Francis let him see, touch, and bind up these holy wounds with bandages, so as to lessen the pain and to staunch the constant bleeding, except from Friday evening to Saturday morning, the time of Christ's crucifixion, death, and burial, when Saint

Francis refused to let any bodily or medical concern keep him from bearing the full pain of Christ's Passion in his own body.

There were times when Brother Leo changed the dressings of the wound to his side that Saint Francis would feel such pain that he would place his hand on Brother Leo's chest, and at the touch of these sacred hands, Brother Leo would faint dead to the ground from the sweetness and devotion of heart that he felt.

At the end of this third part, Saint Francis, having observed the Lent of Saint Michael the Archangel, was inspired by God to return to Santa Maria degli Angeli. So he called Brother Masseo and Brother Leo and after speaking to them and giving them instructions, commended the holy mountain to their tending, as he would now be returning to Santa Maria degli Angeli with Brother Leo. And having said this, he took his leave from them and he blessed them in the name of Christ Crucified, conceding to their request that he lay upon them his holy hands, adorned with the glorious and sacred wounds, such that they might see, touch, and kiss them. And leaving them with this consolation, he left and went down from the holy mountain.

Praise to Jesus Christ and to his poor servant Francis. Amen.

IV

In this fourth part, the true love of Christ completely transformed Saint Francis into God and into the image of Christ Crucified, and now more angel than man, having observed the Lent of Saint Michael the Archangel upon the holy Mount Alverno, Saint Francis came down from the mountain with Brother Leo and with the faithful peasant upon whose donkey he rode, since the nails in his feet did not allow him to walk very well.

Having now come down from the mountain, word of Saint Francis's extraordinary holiness went out throughout the region by way of the shepherds who had seen Mount Alverno on fire as a sign of the great miracle accomplished by God, and upon receiving word of his traveling near by, people from every part of the countryside would flock to see him, men and women, young and old, and inspired with great devotion and love, they sought to touch him and to kiss his hands. Unable to refuse this devotion on people's part but needing to keep his palms bandaged as well as to keep the stigmata hidden from view, he pulled his sleeves down over his hands so that only his fingers showed, and these they kissed.

However, no matter how carefully he attempted to conceal the mystery of these glorious wounds so as to avoid any type of worldly vanity, it was God's will that his glory be manifested in many miracles by virtue of these glorious Sacred Stigmata. Saint Francis's secret and wondrous virtue, his boundless charity, and Christ's mercy on him, with which he had been so wondrously endowed, was shown forth by many clear and evident miracles, in particular on Saint Francis's return from Mount Alverno to Santa Maria degli Angeli but also in various places throughout the world, during his lifetime and after his death, some of which will now be recounted.

Nearing a small village on the outskirts of the area around Arezzo, Saint Francis was approached by a woman carrying her son in her arms and weeping loudly. The boy was eight years old and had suffered for four years with dropsy. So swollen was his stomach that if he stood, he could not see his own feet, and placing her child before Saint Francis, she asked him to pray to God for her son. After first doing as she asked and praying for a time over him, Saint Francis placed his holy hands on the boy's stomach and at once, the swelling disappeared and the boy was restored to health. The woman joyfully hugged her son, and sending him back to their house, she thanked the Lord and his holy saint and invited everyone throughout the countryside to come to her house and see that her son had been cured.

That same day, Saint Francis passed through the town of Borgo San Sepolcro. As he drew near to the castle, an enormous throng came out to meet him from within the castle and the nearby town, waving palm branches before him and shouting loudly, "The holy man is here! The holy man is here!" Spurred on by devotion and eagerness, they crowded all around him to touch him, but though he was touched, grabbed, and pulled every which way, his soul was so rapt in contemplation of God that he neither heard nor felt a single thing that occurred to him that day and was not even aware that he had passed by the castle or the town. After he had gone on his way and everyone in the crowd had gone home, he drew near to a house about a mile outside of the town where lepers were living, and this heavenly contemplative then asked, "How far is it yet to town?" His soul, so fixed and enraptured in contemplation of divine truths, had not perceived any of the earthly events that had taken place. He was unaware of where he had been, how much time had gone by, or anyone who had seen him. This occurred many times, according to the witness of his companions.

That night, Saint Francis came to the community house of the friars at Monte Casale, in which there lived a friar who

was so seriously ill and in such extreme agony from his illness that it seemed he was being tormented by the Evil One
rather than merely suffering from normal sickness. He
would often fall to the ground, seized by a fearsome trembling, foaming from the mouth, as if every nerve in his body
was being stretched and pulled or twisted, such that he
would leap up from the ground only to fall back down
again and again. While at supper, Saint Francis heard of this
brother's miserable and incurable illness from the friars, and
he felt compassion for him. So he took a slice of bread that
he was eating, made the sign of the cross upon it with his
hands bearing the wounds of Christ, and sent it to the ailing
brother who, upon eating the bread, was completely healed
and never suffered again from his illness.

The following morning, Saint Francis sent two of the
brothers from that house to go live on Mount Alverno, and
with them, he sent the peasant who had lent him his donkey
throughout this journey so that he might return to his own
home.

As the two brothers and the peasant made their way
through the countryside around Arezzo, certain of the townspeople saw them and went out to meet them joyfully, thinking it was Saint Francis, who had passed by that way two days
before. Among them was a woman who had been in labor for
three days, and being unable to deliver, she was close to
death. The townspeople thought that she might be freed from
her suffering and cured if Saint Francis were to lay hands
upon her, and they took her to the friars, only to discover to
their dismay that Saint Francis was not among them. And yet,
though Saint Francis was not physically present, the townspeople did not lose their faith. That is when a miracle hap-

pened. The woman looked as if she might die at any moment, and they asked the friars if they had in their possession anything the holy hands of Saint Francis had touched. After thoroughly searching through everything they had with them, they could find nothing except the halter of the donkey upon which he had ridden. Taking therefore this halter with great reverence and devotion and placing it on the woman's body, she called out the name of Saint Francis reverently and put herself under his protection. What happened? As soon as the halter touched the woman, she was rescued from all danger, easily gave birth to her child, and her health was restored.

Saint Francis stayed on in Monte Casale for several days, after which he left and went to Città del Castello, where many of the townspeople brought before him a woman who had long been possessed by an evil spirit, humbly imploring him to free her, for her agonized screams, harsh shouting, and constant howling gave the town no peace. So Saint Francis, after first praying and then making the sign of the cross upon her, commanded the evil spirit to depart from her, which it did at once, leaving her healthy once again in mind and body.

As word of this miracle spread among the people, a woman of great faith brought to Saint Francis her small son, who was suffering from a large and painful ulcer, and asked him to bless her son with his hands. Saint Francis, seeing her faith, took the child, removed the bandages covering the ulcer, and blessed it three times with the sign of the cross, after which he replaced the bandages and returned the child to his mother. As it was evening, she took him home immediately afterward and put him bed. In the morning, she went to awaken him and found that his bandages had been removed and that his ulcer was entirely healed, almost as if it had never been there in the first place, except that where it had been, there was now on his skin the image of a red rose as a sign of the miracle that had taken place. For the rest of his life, he bore the sign of this rose on his skin which often evoked in him great devotion to Saint Francis who had cured him.

Saint Francis spent a month there at the invitation of the faithful townspeople, during which time he performed many other miracles before leaving to return to Santa Maria degli Angeli with Brother Leo and a good man who lent him his donkey to ride.

It so happened, however, that due to bad roads and cold weather, they walked the entire day without coming to any place suitable to stay, and thus, constrained to spend the night outdoors in the bad weather, they took shelter beneath a rock that had been hollowed out and waited out the night, hoping it would stop snowing. Inadequately dressed and very uncomfortable in such conditions, the man who had lent them the donkey was unable to get to sleep (not to mention they had no fire with which to warm themselves), and so, complaining loudly to himself, he began to weep and mutter resentfully against Saint Francis, who had brought them all there. Hearing all this, Saint Francis had compassion on the man, and in a fervor of spirit, reached out, and placed his hand on the man and touched him. Miracle of miracles! As soon as he had touched him with that hand enflamed and pierced by the seraph's fire, all the cold left and the man was pervaded with such warmth that it felt to him as if he stood at the mouth of a roaring furnace, whereupon he fell fast asleep, comforted in body and soul. As he tells it, he slept more peacefully that night among the rocks in the snow than he had ever slept even in his own bed.

They continued their journey forward and came to Santa Maria degli Angeli. As they approached, Brother Leo lifted up his eyes, looked toward this holy spot, and saw before them a beautiful cross, upon which was the body of the Crucified, which moved before Saint Francis, stopping when he stopped, proceeding in front of him as he proceeded forward. So splendid was this cross that not only did it illuminate Saint Francis's own face but cast its light all about the road as they walked, until Saint Francis entered the town of Santa Maria degli Angeli.

Once there, Saint Francis and Brother Leo were received with much rejoicing and affection by the friars, and from that time forward, Saint Francis spent most of the rest of his life there, at Santa Maria degli Angeli, until his death. And as his reputation for sanctity and the stories of his many miracles continued to spread throughout the Order and the world, he tried to hide as much as possible behind his deep humility the many gifts and graces he had received from God, accusing himself at all times of being the most miserable of sinners.

Astounded by this behavior, Brother Leo thought foolishly to himself once, "Imagine him calling himself the most miserable of sinners in public, while his fame grows in the Order and he is more esteemed by the Lord every day. And yet, privately, never does he confess any carnal sin. Is it possible he is still a virgin?" And on this particular matter, he soon became intensely curious to know the truth but dared not ask Saint Francis himself. So he turned to God, asking him to reveal to him the answer to his question, and after much time in prayer, his request was granted by the Lord who showed him in a vision that indeed, Saint Francis was a virgin in his body. In this vision, he saw Saint Francis standing in a high and splendid place, so high that no one else could reach it, and it was revealed to him in spirit that this high and splendid place represented the virginal chastity of Saint Francis, which made complete sense in that his flesh was to be adorned with the Sacred Stigmata of Christ.

Noticing that as time went on, he began to lose more and more of his strength due to the stigmata and soon would no longer be able to direct the Order, Saint Francis quickly called a meeting of the general chapter. When the brothers had gathered all together, he humbly asked forgiveness from the friars that his ill health no longer permitted him to direct the Order or carry out the duties of the general, though he would not and could not resign from this office because he had been made general by the Pope and could not leave office nor appoint a successor without the Pope's express approval. So he made Pietro Cattani his Vicar and affectionately entrusted the welfare of the Order to him and to all the provincial ministers.

Having done this, Saint Francis was at greater peace and, raising his eyes and hands to heaven, said the following, "My Lord and my God, to you I entrust your family, whom you once entrusted to me and of whom now, due to my infirmities, as well you know, my sweet Lord, I can no longer take care. I entrust to you my provincial ministers. To you they will answer on the day of judgment, if due to their negligence or bad example or overly harsh discipline, a single friar is lost." And it pleased God to reveal to all the friars attending the chapter that what Saint Francis was calling his infirmities was in truth his way of referring to the stigmata, and none of them could hold back their tears of devotion. From that time onward, he left all the care and administration of the Order in the hands of his Vicar and provincial ministers, saying, "Because I am no longer able to take care of the Order due to my infirmities, I now have only my prayers to the Lord to offer for the good of our Order and to set an example for our friars. Indeed, I know, even if this infirmity were to leave me, the greatest help I could render to the Order would be to pray continually that the Lord defend, rule, and protect it."

As has been said before, Saint Francis took great care, as much as he could, to hide the Sacred Stigmata, going about with his hands and feet bandaged, but from this point forward, he could not stop many of the friars from wanting to see and touch him, especially the wound in his side, which he took particular care to keep hidden. Thus, there was a time when a brother who was tending to him persuaded him, respectfully and carefully, to remove his tunic so that he might clean it, and taking it off in his presence, he clearly saw the wound in his side and with a deft touch, placed three fingers upon it so as to judge its size and depth. In the same way, his Vicar was among those who saw this wound as well. But it was Brother Ruffino whose testimony is the surest, a man of great contemplative gifts about whom many times Saint Francis had said no holier man was there on earth, whose sanctity Saint Francis dearly loved, and to whom Saint Francis granted whatever he desired.

Three separate times did Brother Ruffino along with others verify the presence of the stigmata, particularly the wound in his side. The first time was when he was washing Saint Francis's underclothes, which he wore especially loose and high so that he might cover the wound on his right side. Looking at these underclothes carefully and examining them, he found that they were always bloody on the right side, which confirmed that the wound was bleeding there. However, when Saint Francis caught him laying out his underclothes in this way in order to discover proof of his wound, he admonished Brother Ruffino. The second time he was scratching Saint Francis's back and carefully ran his hand around Saint Francis's side and put a finger into the wound, at which Saint Francis cried out in pain and said, "God forgive you, Brother Ruffino. Why did you do that?" The third time was when Brother Ruffino asked Saint Francis the favor of exchanging habits with him, out of fraternal love and charity. Reluctantly granting Brother Ruffino this favor, the beloved father removed his habit and gave it to Brother Ruffino, who gave Saint Francis his own, and in this exchange, Brother Ruffino could clearly see the wound.

Brother Leo and many other friars also saw the Sacred Stigmata on Saint Francis during his lifetime, and though they are men of faith and holiness whose word ought to be trusted without question, they nevertheless wish to banish any doubt and thus swear on sacred Scripture that they did indeed see the wounds with their own eyes. Several cardinals who were on familiar terms with Saint Francis likewise saw the wounds and in reverence have written beautiful, devout hymns, antiphons, and verses concerning them. The sovereign pontiff, Pope Alexander, preaching to the people in the presence of all the cardinals (among whose number was Saint Bonaventure, friar and cardinal), stated that he had seen the Sacred Stigmata of Saint Francis during his lifetime. Lady Jacopa of Settesoli in Roma, greatest noblewoman in Rome at the time and profoundly devoted to Saint Francis, also saw them before his death, and after his death, saw and kissed them several times out of reverence, having come, by divine revelation, from Rome to Assisi to be with Saint Francis as he died, as is recounted here.

Saint Francis, a few days before his death, lay ill in the palace of the bishop of Assisi, accompanied by friends, and all throughout his illness, he would sing certain praises of Christ. One day, one of his companions said to him, "Father, you know the townspeople have great faith in you and consider you a holy man, and so they think that if you are who they think you are, you ought to be thinking about the fact you are about to die and rather than singing, you ought to be weeping over how seriously ill you are. You need to realize that our singing here can be heard through the palace, which is being guarded by armed men, and they may well take offense at our behavior, given how sick you are. So, it's my opinion," said this friar, "that you would do well to leave this place and return to Santa Maria degli Angeli, for we may not fare well here among these laymen."

Saint Francis answered him, saying, "Dearest brother, you know that two years ago, when we were staying in Foligno, the Lord revealed to you the hour of my death as he did to me as well, and in a few days, by reason of this illness, that hour will soon arrive. In this revelation, the Lord gave me assurance of the forgiveness of all my sins and of heaven's blessing. During this revelation, I wept then for my sins and for my death, but since then, I am so filled with happiness that I can no longer weep. So I sing and I will continue to sing to God who has given me the great richness of his grace and has assured me of my entry to heaven. I agree with you and wish to take leave from here now. Only you will have to find a way to carry me, since I am too ill to make it on my own." So the brothers took him in their arms and carried him, accompanied by many townspeople.

Passing by a hospital on one of the streets of the town,

Saint Francis said to those who were carrying him, "Lay me down here and turn me toward the town." They placed him with his face turned to Assisi, and Saint Francis blessed the town many times, saying, "Blessed by God are you, holy city! Many souls will be saved in you, in you many servants of God will live, and in you many will be chosen for the kingdom of eternal life." Having said this, Saint Francis was carried away to Santa Maria degli Angeli.

Arriving at Santa Maria degli Angeli, they took him to the infirmary and laid him down to rest. Then Saint Francis called one of his companions to himself and said to him, "Beloved Brother, the Lord has shown me that I will pass from this life in a few days due to this illness, and you know that if Lady Jacopa of Settesoli, beloved and devoted to our Order, knew of my death and was not here with me, she would be deeply aggrieved. So tell her that, if she wishes to see me, she should come to me immediately."

The friar answered, "Very true, Father, given her devotion to you, she would be disconsolate if she were not here at your death."

"Go, then," said Saint Francis, "bring pen, paper, and inkwell and write down what I tell you," and when all was brought to his bedside, he dictated the following letter:

"To Lady Jacopa, servant of God, Saint Francis, poor man of Christ, sends his greetings in the fellowship of the Holy Spirit in our Lord Jesus Christ. Please know, beloved, that our beloved Christ by his grace has shown me the end of my life, which will be soon. So, if you wish to see me while I live, upon receipt of this letter, do not delay and come to Santa Maria degli Angeli, for if you cannot come right away, then you may not find me alive. And when you come, bring with you some haircloth to wrap my body and some wax to be used in my burial. And I ask you to bring also some of the food you used to give me when I was ill in Rome."

While writing this letter, God revealed to Saint Francis that Lady Jacopa was already on her way to him and that she was quite near to the community house, bringing all the things he had been asking her to bring. So Saint Francis told the friar who had been writing that he need not continue writing any more since there was no need, and that he could put the letter away. The friars in attendance were amazed at his behavior, since he didn't finish the letter and did not want it to be sent. But after a short time, there was a loud knock on the door to the house and Saint Francis sent the doorman to open it. There stood Lady Jacopa, greatest noblewoman of Rome, along with two of her sons, who were senators, and a great retinue of men on horseback, all of whom came in.

Lady Jacopa went straight to the infirmary to the side of Saint Francis, who rejoiced and was much consoled in her having come, and she rejoiced as well in her turn, seeing him alive and speaking with him. At that time she told him of the way God had revealed to her, while praying in Rome, that he did not have long to live and that he would send for her and ask her to bring certain things, all of which she did in fact bring with her. She sent for these things and began to feed him with the food he had requested, and after he had eaten and was more comfortable, Lady Jacopa knelt at his most holy feet, adorned with the wounds of Christ, held them in her hands, and with boundless devotion, kissed them and bathed them with her tears, seeming to the friars in attendance like Mary Magdalene herself at the feet of Christ, such that they dared not try to take her from him.

Finally, after a long time, they helped her up and took her aside, asking her how she had come so fortuitously and so well supplied with the very things that Saint Francis required in his illness and for his burial. Lady Jacopa answered them that, while praying one night, she heard a voice from heaven saying, "If you wish to see Saint Francis alive, go without delay to Assisi and take with you the food you used to give him when he was ill and the things that will be needed for his burial." So that, she said, is what I did.

Lady Jacopa stayed with Saint Francis until he had died and was buried, and she, with all her retinue, paid him great homage at his burial and saw to all the expenses that were required. Shortly after her return to Rome, this blessed lady died a very holy death, and out of devotion to Saint Francis, had made provision to be taken and buried at Santa Maria degli Angeli, which was done according to her wishes.

On the death of Saint Francis, not only Lady Jacopa and her sons and their retinue beheld and kissed his glorious Sacred Stigmata, but also many townspeople of Assisi did as well, among whom was a very well-known and prominent knight, by the name of Jerome, who held many doubts about the reports and refused to believe, much like Saint Thomas the Apostle. To convince himself and others, right in front of the friars and other laypeople, he was so bold as to actually move the nails in the hands and feet of Saint Francis and ran his hand over the wounds. Thus, he became a reliable witness to the truth of the accounts, swearing on the Bible that he had indeed seen and touched the wounds.

Saint Clare and her sisters also saw and kissed the Sacred Stigmata of Saint Francis and were present at his burial.

Praise be to Jesus Christ and his poor servant Saint Francis. Amen.

Saint Francis, glorious confessor of Christ, passed from this life in the year of our Lord 1226, on Saturday, October 4, and was buried the following day, on Sunday. That year was the twentieth anniversary of his conversion, that is, when he repented of his former life, and the second year following the imposition of the Sacred Stigmata. He was forty-five years old.

Praise be to Jesus Christ and his poor servant Saint Francis. Amen.

Saint Francis was canonized in the year 1228, by Pope Gregory IX, who came in person to Assisi for the canonization.

Praise be to Jesus Christ and his poor servant Saint Francis. Amen.

V

This is the fifth and last part, concerning certain apparitions, revelations, and miracles that the Lord accomplished and made manifest after the death of Saint Francis so as to confirm that Saint Francis had received the Sacred Stigmata and to reveal the day and the hour when Christ had granted them to him.

In the year of our Lord 1282, in the month of October, Brother Filippo, minister of Tuscany, on the order of Brother Bongrazia, minister general of the Order, asked Brother Matteo of Castiglione Aretino, a very devout and holy man, to tell him what he knew of the day and the hour in which the Sacred Stigmata had been imprinted by Christ on the body of Saint Francis, because he had heard that Brother Matteo had

had a revelation about it. Under holy obedience, Brother Matteo replied:

"While living in the community on Mount Alverno this past year, in the month of May, I began to pray in the cell in which it is believed that the seraph appeared to Saint Francis, and during my prayers, I prayed earnestly to God that he might be pleased to reveal to someone the day, hour, and place in which the Sacred Stigmata were imprinted upon the body of Saint Francis. I persisted in prayer well into the early hours of the morning, and Saint Francis appeared to me within a great light and said to me, 'My son, what are you asking the Lord for?' And I said to him, 'Holy Father, you know what I am praying for.' And he said to me, 'I am your Father Francis, do you recognize me?' I said, 'Yes, I do.'

"He then showed me the Sacred Stigmata on his hands, feet, and side and said to me, 'The time has now come when it pleases God to manifest his glory by revealing to the friars what, up to now, they had not sought to know. What appeared to me was not an angel, but Jesus Christ in the form of a seraph whose hands imprinted upon my body the five wounds he himself had received upon his body on the cross. And it happened in this manner: the day before the Feast of the Holy Cross, an angel came to me and told me to prepare myself to receive patiently that which God was pleased to give me. The following morning, that is, on the Feast of the Holy Cross, which was on a Friday that year, I rose and left my cell at dawn in a great fervor of spirit and came to pray here in this spot where you are now, a place where I often came to pray. And in praying, I saw a crucified young man in the form of a seraph with six wings rapidly descending in the air before me from heaven. Before this wondrous sight, I humbly fell to my knees and began to devoutly contemplate the boundless love of Jesus Christ Crucified and the boundless suffering in his Passion. His appearance evoked in me such compassion that it seemed to me that I felt his Passion in my own body, and from his presence, the entire mountain shone with a light as brilliant as the sun. Having come down close down in front of me, he told me certain secret things that I have not yet ever revealed to anyone, but the time is approaching when these things shall be revealed. And then, after some time, Christ departed and ascended into heaven, and I found myself marked with these wounds. Go then,' said Saint Francis, 'and tell these things with certainty to your minister, for God, and not man, has done these things.' And having said these words, Saint Francis blessed me and ascended into heaven with a great multitude of radiant youths."

This is the account that Brother Matteo gave of what he had seen and heard while waking during his vigil and that he swore to before the minister in Florence, in his cell, when asked to do so under obedience.

Praise be to Jesus Christ and his poor servant Saint Francis. Amen.

How one holy friar, reading about the Sacred Stigmata in the story of Saint Francis and about the secrets told him by the seraph when he appeared to Saint Francis, prayed to the Lord that Saint Francis might reveal these secrets to him.

One day, a devout and holy friar was reading the story of Saint Francis, and having gotten to the part concerning the Sacred Stigmata, began to feel in his spirit a great eagerness to know what those secrets were that had been spoken to Saint Francis when the Seraph had appeared to him and that he had never revealed to anyone during his lifetime. He said to himself, "Saint Francis did not wish to reveal these words to anyone while he lived, but perhaps now he might, after his death, if someone earnestly prayed that he do so." So this devout friar began to pray to the Lord and to Saint Francis that they might be willing to reveal these secrets, and having persevered in this prayer over the course of eight years, his prayer was at last granted in the following fashion:

One day, after eating and giving thanks in church, this friar was praying more earnestly than usual and with many tears to the Lord and to Saint Francis in one part of the church, when he was called by another friar, on the order of the guardian, to accompany him into town on community business. Knowing that obedience was far more worthy than prayer, he responded immediately to the prelate's order, left off his prayers, and went humbly to the friar who had called to him. And it was God's will that this simple act of prompt obedience made him worthy of what eight long years of prayer till then had not. No sooner were they out the door of the community house when they came upon two friars who seemed to be from a foreign country. One of the friars was young, the other more aged and thin, and due to bad weather, they were covered in mud and soaking wet. Seeing this and feeling compassion for the two of them, the obedient friar said to the companion going to town with him, "Beloved brother, could we not put off the errand we are running, since these two foreigners are in great need of our charity? Allow me to go first and wash their feet, especially the older one who truly needs it, and you can wash the feet of the younger one. Then we can go about our errand for the community." Agreeing with his companion's charitable impulse, they went back into the house and took these two foreign friars in, bringing them into the kitchen near the hearth, where eight of the other brothers already were, so they could get warm and dry for a time.

After sitting a while before the fire, they took them aside and washed their feet, as they had previously planned, and as the obedient friar washed away the great deal of mud that covered the feet of the older brother, he saw the marks of the stigmata. With joy and wonder, he embraced them at once and began to shout, "Either you are Christ or you are Saint Francis." Hearing his exclamation, all the other brothers around the hearth leapt up and gathered about, with fear and reverence, to see the glorious stigmata, which, in response to their requests, the older brother permitted them to see, touch, and kiss. And as they were filled with wonder and happiness, he said to them, "Have no fears or doubts, my dearest brothers and sons, I am indeed Brother Francis, your spiritual father, who, by the will of God, founded three Orders. I have been asked in prayer, for eight years now, by the friar who is washing my feet—and who asked in an especially earnest way this very day—to reveal the secret words that the seraph spoke to me when he gave me these stigmata, the secrets that I never wanted to reveal during my life on earth. But today, by God's command and in answer to this friar's perseverance and in reward for his obedience, by which he left behind him the sweet pleasure of his contemplative prayer, I have been sent by God to reveal to him, before you, that which he has requested."

Saint Francis then turned to the friar and said, "Beloved Brother, when I was on Mount Alverno, my spirit totally taken up in remembrance of the Passion of Christ, I was given these stigmata by the seraphic apparition of Christ, and Christ said to me, 'Do you know what I have done for you? I have given you the stigmata that are the signs of my Passion, so that you will be my standard-bearer. Just as I, on the day of my death, went down into the underworld and rescued the souls there by virtue of my wounds, so, too, on the day of your death, you may rescue all the souls of the three Orders, Friars Minors, Sisters, and the Penitents, and all the others who had in their lives been devoted to you, raising them up to the glory of heaven by virtue of your wounds. In your death you may be conformed to me, as you were in your life." These are the words that I never spoke to anyone while I lived.

And having said these words, Saint Francis and his companion disappeared. Many brothers heard this account from the eight brothers would had been present to this vision and to the words Saint Francis spoke that day.

Praise be to Jesus Christ and his poor servant Saint Francis. Amen.

How Saint Francis, after his death, appeared to Brother John of Alverno while he was in prayer.

On Mount Alverno, Saint Francis once appeared to Brother John of Alverno, a man of great holiness, while he was in prayer, and he stayed with him and spoke to him for a long time, and in the end, wishing to depart, Saint Francis said to him, "Tell me what you would like."

Brother John said, "Father, I ask you to tell me something that I have longed to know for quite some time: what were you doing and where were you when the seraph appeared to you?"

Saint Francis answered him, saying, "I was praying in that

place where there now stands the chapel of Count Simon of Battifolle, and I was praying that our Lord Jesus Christ might grant me two graces. The first was that, while I was alive, I might feel within my soul and my body, as deeply as possible, the pain that he had felt when his suffering in the Passion was at its worst. The second grace I was requesting was that I might feel in my heart the extraordinary love that enflamed him to suffer this passion for us sinners. At which the Lord put into my heart the knowledge that he would grant me the grace to feel both, as much as is possible for a mortal man, and this was accomplished through the imprint of the stigmata." Then Brother John asked him if the secret words that the seraph had spoken to him were indeed the same as had been spoken to the friar around the fire and affirmed as having been heard in the presence of the eight other friars, his companions. Saint Francis replied that, yes, they were, and that the friar was speaking the truth.

So Brother John felt confident enough in the generosity of his patron to then say, "Oh Father, I beg you at this very moment to let me see and kiss your glorious stigmata, not because I have doubts but rather so that I might be consoled, for this is something I have always desired." Saint Francis generously showed him the wounds and offered them to him, whereby Brother John saw, touched, and kissed them. Finally, Brother John said, "Father, what consolation your soul must have felt as Christ blessed you and granted you these marks of his most holy Passion! May God be pleased to grant such sweet consolation to me as well!"

Saint Francis answered this, saying, "Do you see these nails?" and Brother John said, "Yes, Father." Saint Francis said, "Then touch once more the nail that I have in my hand."

Brother John with deep reverence and awe touched the nail, and as he touched it, a fragrance was released like a puff of smoke or incense, and smelling this fragrance, Brother John's body and soul were filled with such a sweetness that he became rapt in ecstasy and lost his senses, and he stayed in this state from morning prayer until Vespers. Brother John never revealed this vision or this intimate conversation with Saint Francis to anyone other than his confessor until he was on his deathbed, whereupon he recounted it to certain brothers.

Praise be to Jesus Christ and his poor servant Saint Francis. Amen.

Concerning a holy brother who saw a miraculous vision of a companion of his who had died.

In the province of Rome, a very devout and holy brother saw the following miraculous vision. A day after the death of one of the more beloved of his brothers within his community, who was buried under the entryway to the chapter house, this friar was seated in the corner of the entryway after dinner praying to the Lord and to Saint Francis for the soul of his deceased brother. And going deeply into prayer with many tears until noontime, as the other friars went to nap, he heard a great noise throughout the cloister that frightened him greatly. He turned his eyes to the tomb of his companion and saw Saint Francis standing there, and behind him, a great multitude of friars gathered around the tomb. Beyond them he could see, in the middle of the cloister, a large flame of fire, and in the midst of this flame was the soul of the deceased brother. Looking around the cloister, he saw Jesus Christ walking around the cloister with a great company of angels and saints.

Beholding these things with amazement, he saw that when

Christ passed by the entryway, Saint Francis and all the friars with him knelt down and said, "I beg you, dear Lord and Father, through that inestimable charity that you have shown to the human race by your incarnation, that you show mercy to the soul of this, my brother, who is burning in the fire." Christ said nothing but continued to walk. As Christ came around a second time, passing by the entryway again, Saint Francis knelt down with the rest of the friars, as he had the first time, and said the following, "I beg you, merciful Lord and Father, for the charity without measure that you have shown to the human race by the wood of your cross; have mercy on the soul of this, my brother." And Christ once again passed by without responding. As Christ made the round of the cloister one more time and came back a third time and passed by the entryway, Saint Francis, kneeling as he had before, showed him his hands, feet, and chest, saying, "I beg you, merciful Lord and Father, by the great suffering and even greater consolation that I was granted when you imprinted this stigmata upon my flesh, have mercy on the soul of this, my brother, in the fire of purgatory." Wonder of wonders! Having been implored a third time by Saint Francis in the name of his stigmata, Christ halted and looked down at the stigmata, granted the prayer, and said, "To you, Brother Francis, I give the soul of your brother," thus honoring and confirming the Sacred Stigmata of Saint Francis and clearly intending to show that the souls of any friars in purgatory would be most easily be freed from their suffering and lifted to the glory of paradise by virtue of the stigmata. At once, the flame in the middle of the cloister disappeared, and the deceased friar went to Saint Francis, and with him and with Christ, along with the whole of their blessed and glorious company, ascended into heaven.

Having been granted what he had prayed for on behalf of his companion and seeing him freed from suffering and lifted to paradise, the friar rejoiced greatly and recounted the entire vision to other brothers in the Order, and with them, he praised and gave thanks to the Lord.

Praise be to Jesus Christ and his poor servant Saint Francis. Amen.

How a noble knight, devoted to Saint Francis, received assurance of his death and of the stigmata of Saint Francis.

A noble knight of Massa di San Piero, named Sir Landulf, deeply devoted to Saint Francis, who invested him with the habit of the Third Order, was assured of Saint Francis's death and of his glorious stigmata in the following way:

Hearing that Saint Francis was near to death, the Evil One took possession of a woman living in the castle, tormenting her most cruelly and giving her the facility to speak with such subtlety and learning that she argued successfully against even the most educated and wise men who came to dispute with her. For two days, the demon would leave her, but on the third day it would again possess her and afflict her even more cruelly than before. Hearing of this possession, Sir Landulf went to the woman and asked the demon who possessed her why it was that he would depart for two days and then return on the third to torment her more cruelly than before. The demon answered him, saying, "When I left her, it was so that I could join with my companions nearby and go with even greater power to attend to Saint Francis, who was dying, to take possession of his soul. But since his soul was surrounded and so strongly defended by an even greater multitude of angels, who outnumbered us and who accompanied him directly to heaven, we left there confounded, and I came back here to torment this poor woman whom I had left for two days."

So Sir Landulf enjoined him in the name of God to tell him the truth regarding the sanctity of Saint Francis, who had died, and of Saint Clare, who was still living. The demon answered, saying, "I shall tell you the truth, whether I want to or not. God the Father was once so offended by the sinfulness of this world that for a brief time he had wanted to render a final judgment upon all men and women and wipe them from the face of the earth, if they did not repent. But his son Christ, praying on behalf of sinners, promised that he would recreate his life and his Passion in one man, namely, the poor beggar Francis, whose life and teaching would lead many in the world back to the way of truth and to a conversion of life. And now, in order to show the world what he has done in Saint Francis, he has desired that the stigmata of his Passion, the marks that he imprinted upon Saint Francis's body during his life, would now, after his death, be seen and touched by many people. In like fashion, the Mother of Christ promised to renew her virginal purity and humility in one woman, namely, Saint Clare, by whose example many thousands of women would escape from our evil clutches. And thus, by virtue of these promises, God the Father showed mercy and set aside his final judgment."

Sir Landulf, wishing to know for certain if the demon, storehouse and father of all manner of deceit, was indeed telling the truth, especially with regard to the death of Saint Francis, sent one of his faithful servants to Santa Maria degli Angeli at Assisi to inquire whether Saint Francis was alive or had died, and the servant, upon his arrival, discovered that all was as the demon had said. The servant returned to his lord with this news, that the very day and time that the demon had told him was when Saint Francis had passed from this life.

Praise be to Jesus Christ and his poor servant Saint Francis. Amen.

How Pope Gregory IX, doubting the stigmata of Saint Francis, was enlightened on the matter.

In addition to all the miracles attached to the Sacred Stigmata of Saint Francis that are recounted in the story of his life, this fifth and last part of our account will end with Pope Gregory IX who, having some doubts about the wound in Saint Francis's side, recounts the following.

One night Saint Francis appeared to Pope Gregory IX, and lifting his right arm up, he showed him the wound in his side and asked him for a flask, which he fetched. Saint Francis placed the flask beneath his wound and the Pope could see it being filled to the brim with blood and water flowing from the wound. From that point onward, he had no further doubts, and so, with the cardinals, gave his approval to the Sacred Stigmata of Saint Francis, granting to the friars the special privileges of a bull, published in Viterbo in the eleventh year of his pontificate, and in the year 1300 he published another bull with even more privileges.

Pope Nicholas III and Pope Alexander IV likewise granted

further privileges, such that whosoever should deny the stigmata of Saint Francis would be prosecuted as one would prosecute a heretic.

And this is the end of the fifth part of the account of the Sacred Stigmata of our father Saint Francis, whose life the Lord gave us as an example to follow in this world, and by virtue of whose glorious stigmata we might be made worthy to share paradise with him.

Praise be to Jesus Christ and his poor servant Saint Francis. Amen.

APPENDIX: CHAPTER NUMBERING OF THE *FIORETTI*

The following chart gives the correspondence between the chapter numbers in this abridged edition and the original numbering of chapters in the *Fioretti*.

This Edition	Original Edition
1	1
2	2
3	3
4	4
5	5
6	6
7	7
8	8
9	9
10	11
11	13
12	14
13	15
14	16
15	17